The Theatre Student

COURT AND COMMEDIA
The Italian Renaissance Stage

The Theatre Student

COURT AND COMMEDIA
The Italian Renaissance Stage

David Brubaker

PUBLISHED BY

RICHARDS ROSEN PRESS, INC.
NEW YORK, N.Y. 10010

Published in 1975 by Richards Rosen Press, Inc.
29 East 21st Street, New York, N.Y. 10010

FIRST EDITION

Library of Congress Cataloging in Publication Data

Brubaker, David.
   Court and commedia.

   (The Theatre student series)
   Bibliography: p.
   Includes index.
   1. Performing arts—Italy—History. I. Title.
PN2679.B78   790.2'0945   75–8965
ISBN 0–8239–0317–6

Manufactured in the United States of America

To charming lady Marj, this dedication.
To Darrell, my obedient son.
To those in higher education
Who do their thing at Dickinson.

And let the rhymes upon this page
Salute companions of the stage.
Praise all that made the Green Room scene
Or were at Ebensberg or Keene,
The Erie year, the Cleveland season.
Applaud who played the Traverse region
And those who did Chautauquan things
Or paid their dues at Boiling Springs.
If in Japan they made their faces
Or were in less exotic places,
I thank them all. And Hollywood?
Even that, at last, if least, was good.

ABOUT THE AUTHOR

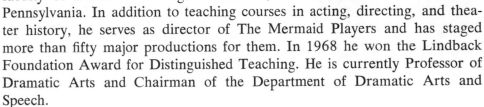

DAVID BRUBAKER grew up in Lancaster, Pennsylvania. He received an A.B. degree from Franklin and Marshall College in Lancaster and began his acting career with the college Green Room Club, under the direction of Darrell Larsen. A professional actor and member of Actors' Equity Association since 1947, he appeared in character and leading roles in more than 150 productions in repertory at The Cleveland Playhouse, The Erie Playhouse, and in stock theaters in Pennsylvania, New York, New England, Florida, and Michigan.

In 1956 Professor Brubaker joined the faculty of Dickinson College in Carlisle, Pennsylvania. In addition to teaching courses in acting, directing, and theater history, he serves as director of The Mermaid Players and has staged more than fifty major productions for them. In 1968 he won the Lindback Foundation Award for Distinguished Teaching. He is currently Professor of Dramatic Arts and Chairman of the Department of Dramatic Arts and Speech.

Marj Green Brubaker, Professor Brubaker's wife, is a professional stage designer who has created settings for stock and community theaters. For the past ten years, she has designed the productions at Dickinson. In 1952 and 1953, while Professor Brubaker was on active duty in the Navy, they were able to study the Japanese Kabuki theater at first hand. In Japan, too, they adopted their son, Darrell, now a young man of twenty-three.

CONTENTS

The Theatre Student

COURT AND COMMEDIA
The Italian Renaissance Stage

Chapter I

LOOKING BACKWARD

Our topic is the theatre of Renaissance Italy, a theatre whose best achievements were in the showmanship of court spectacle, in the theatricalism of improvised comedy, and in the development of opera. It is a chapter of theatre history neglected by historians of a literary bias for it was not the most notable, if dramatic literature is the measure of notability, and it had, perhaps, too much romance and dazzle for the sobrieties of a lesson plan. In the index of this study, Arlecchino and Aristotle are neighbors and Sophocles keeps company with a Capitano Spavento. But this Italian theatre established and so powerfully changed the theatre of the West that we need the pleasure of its company, the knowledge of what went into it, if we are to understand our theatre and its peculiar ways.

We begin with the obvious: actors, dramatists, scenic artists, audiences, and patrons make a work of theatre art. If we want to know theatre, we need to know the makers of theatre and how they influence one another. It seems simple, but in the same way a performance hides its complexity (that being what rehearsals are for) so the influence of one or another of these elements of the mix is no simple matter to appraise. Each collaborator has his say. As a result, the dramatist, for instance, is not free to simply write. He needs to deal with a workaday series of questions. When does the audience expect to get home from his play? Will it sit at ease or stand at restless attention? The answers will tell him if he should be brief or may be less concise, if he may indulge in a longer legato rhythm or

should use a series of short, varied scenes. He will need to consider the technical resources his theatre has. Should the action be planned, for example, for one setting or may he place things where he wants? If one setting is chosen, will he send the neighbor in his cast of characters into the house to borrow her cup of sugar or out of the house to meet the lender in the street? What charms and skills can he expect his performers to bring to his play? Should his play please the populace to make money or please a patron who will pay the bill? Confronting these and other questions as tiresome, a playwright complained, "In the theatre we are asked to submit to too much." It does not matter that he was Émile Zola or that he penned his protest a hundred years ago; he expressed the thought of many. He felt "hobbled," he wrote, by the theatre's "army of collaborators to which one must submit from the imposing leading man down to the prompter. How much more independent are we in the novel!"

This army of actors, audience, technicians, and patrons has its own concerns and at times feels that it, too, submits to too much. The imposing leading man imposes his worry about how and what he will act. The designer deals in banalities as well as beauty; weights and measures, logistics and economics, as well as composition and color.

Might there be some formula to express how these collaborators submit to one another, a formula defining the complex relationships of theatre art? These relationships are, happily, too slapdash for that and are easier imagined than reduced to word or number. The clout of an individual collaborator varies from time to time, one or another becoming more or less "equal" than the others.

One of these collaborators properly understood and weighed, however, can give us a clue to the others. When the big bus eases into 45th or 46th Street, bringing its geriatric trade to the Broadway matinee, we may guess that something like *Pippin* or *Over Here!* is on the boards. The dramatist can tell us something about his audience; the audience tells us something about the show. If we are canny, we may look sideways from one collaborator to another and glimpse the whole theatre form. And we may look backward to its tradition and make a more educated guess.

There are also certain less human, more abstract, yet potent forces collaborating to make theatre. I refer to the religious, political, social, cultural, and economic forces that are part of the mixture. Each one of these elements exerts a pressure that varies in degree or kind, and as these pressures come together they create the configuration of a distinct theatre form. Theatre is a thing of the moment of performance, but the moment has a history and this seemingly ephemeral thing cannot be understood in any significant way without looking carefully at its collaborators and looking backward to the tradition each expresses in his work.

Because theatre cannot be the work of an individual artist, it is peculiarly responsive to the common ideas held by the group needed to make it. Ideas about the kinds of plays that should be produced, the way they should be performed, and the way they should be staged shape a distinct theatre form. These ideas come from the past. Founded as it is on commonly held conceptions, the theatre is necessarily a conservative institution. Theatrical ideas and practices do not change often or much.

The newest movie house in town has curtains decorating its screen. For what purpose? They are so chintzy that they rule out any aesthetic justification; they do fulfill an odd, old expectation. Similarly, the high school, newly built last year, has a stage equipped with strips of footlights and borders more appropriate to gas illumination than light supplied by electric lamps. There seems no way to account for these things unless we reckon that there is a conservative impulse which decks our movie house and high school stage with things we have come to expect. In the theatre, we seek the resemblance of things past.

Given this backwardness as a fact of theatre life, we are the more interested in those tides of influence which once upon a time produced change in it. Such a time of tide was the period of about 150 years beginning about 1500. The forms and traditions of theatre developed then in Italy have shaped our modern European theatre in ways still perceptible today. That theatre should be indoors and artificially lit, that curtains should be in view before the show—two homely instances of theatrical practice (or, we may say, of things to which we must submit)—had their beginning then and there.

Other less ordinary things, parcels of Western theatrical theory and practice, are of Italian descent and have similar longevity. Opera is, of course, one. Changeable scenery is also Italian. So is the idea that in addition to costumed players and their essential props, stage decoration should include pictorial elements. The way we make scenery of painted cloth stretched over wooden frames is Italian, too. The proscenium arch, recently the subject of second thoughts by our theatre's theorists, was first thought of as the necessary frame for the decor of Italian sixteenth-century stages. The pastoral play was Italian. Also, perhaps more happy to relate in the past tense, were the critical dicta of the three unities in dramaturgy. Still another part of this survey is a unique theatre form, the commedia dell'arte. Once a vital element of European theatre, now a bit softer-spoken and moving less vividly, we see its reflection or hear its echo in contemporary improvisation, in mime and pantomime, and in a gallery of figures with us yet: Punch and Judy, Pierrot and Pierrette, Harlequin and Columbine.

Before we look backward at these Italian Renaissance contributions to our theatrical ideas, expectations, and practice, it is well to consider that the sixteenth-century artists would have done the same. So we should start with a consideration of what their backward look would have brought to their view. What tradition had they?

The theatre of Europe in the late medieval period was a religious theatre. Its subject matter was taken from the Bible and from the stories of saints and martyrs, and it presented a vision of life hallowed by the teachings of the church and its moralists. The given subject matter of the mystery and miracle plays had some embellishments reflecting the life of the time. So did the moralities, which were illustrative teachings concerned with the journey of Mankind or Everyman toward a confrontation with doom or salvation. Allegorical characters—Virtues, Vices, Good Deeds, Right Doctrine, and other abstractions—figured as dramatis personae. Unlike the vapid and rather uninteresting connotation its qualifying adjective now has, this religious theatre encompassed a wide spectrum of human concern. Comedy and horseplay leapt on stage along with the most correct and elevating intimations. It was a theatre of splashy color, marvelous spectacle, and great variety. The plays were the work of anonymous writers and rewriters. Although many of them were short pieces, they were often presented as parts of a cycle that may have taken a day or days to perform. The biblical plays joined creation and the Last Judgment in a comprehensive span. God the Father, the angels in heaven, the world, the flesh, and the devil were all present and accounted for.

The typical staging method of the period employed what we call a simultaneous setting, or multiple staging. Such a staging method requires that all of the settings, called mansions, used for a play or group of plays are in view at one time. A setting of this type was as diverse as the universality of the subject matter would lead one to expect. The actors associated with a particular mansion moved to, entered from, and grouped around it. The scenic properties and structures derived their meaning from the way they were used as often as from what they in fact represented. The surrounding area was considered an unlocalized, neutral place. As an example of this type of staging method, the Passion play performed at Valenciennes may be cited. It had its mansions set out on a long platform, with paradise at one end and hell at the other. Mansions or set pieces between these extremes represented the palace of Herod, the Temple, Nazareth, the Sea of Galilee, and other places needed in the vast cycle of plays. Cities were represented by a mansion that resembled nothing so much as a handsome gate or door, a kind of symbol of the gates of a walled city. The Temple was a raised, open platform with a roof structure and cupola supported by pillars. A practicable ship floated on the sea. Hell was a flaming place with writhing damned souls and dancing imps framed by a huge monster head with gaping jaws. It was a huge structure and from it belched smoke, the clatter of fireworks, and the din of pot-pounding imps. Paradise was a sizable circular construction raised aloft, high above a mansion. God the Father was majestically enthroned and surrounded by a moving circle of angel figures. The mansions set up for a

FIG. 1. *Stage of the Valenciennes Passion play of 1547. Theatre Arts Prints.*

series of plays or scenes may be called settings only if we use the word in the same way we speak of a jewel setting. They were decorative, ornate, and often most elaborate, but they tended to be symbolic structures setting off the scene, providing a focus, rather than locating the scene by means of realistic illusion. The "picture" was a geographic and architectural jumble having the picturesque charm of a giant's toy collection and about as much unity. The medieval stage was diffuse.

A somewhat similar staging method is returning to our theatre today, where it has an experimental air and a certain modishness. Elements of the setting or playing areas are set up variously in the theatre space. This kind of staging was resoundingly successful in Hal Prince's production of *Candide,* a show that won the Drama Critics Award as the best musical of 1974.

There were no regular theatres for the medieval stage, even though performances may have taken place on the same spot each year. The costumes, properties, machinery, paraphernalia needed for trick effects, and mansions were taken from storage and the stage was erected anew each time a cycle was to be performed. Most performances were given in the open air. Sometimes the mansion stage was a long rectangular platform, as at Valenciennes; sometimes the mansions were set out in a semicircular or circular arrangement; and sometimes they were set up at random inside or in front of the church, around a square, or in a marketplace or some open field beyond city walls. Often the mansions were mounted on wagons and became parade floats, which were pulled through the streets in a procession to the playing place. The occasion for a performance was most often an annual holy day, and to celebrate it the mansions would be refurbished and the plays rehearsed again. Their annual repetition suggests they had a kind of ritual significance.

The expertise of this theatre lay in the hands of the men who made the mansions, decorated them, and mastered the tricks of a stagecraft designed to impress the rude gapers who came to see the annual marvel. The actors were amateurs who left their usual labors for the time it took to prepare and perform the plays. Obviously, the motive was religious and this theatre was created for the instruction of the unlettered and for the glory of God. A carefully rehearsed and impressively staged cycle, however, attracted people from some distance away and had a commercial value to the trade guilds, which mounted the plays in many towns.

There was quite a bit of less regular and less reverent theatre activity in Europe during the late medieval period. Fraternal groups and student societies amused themselves with performances of farces and interludes. Courts and even monasteries had entertainments that included plays. The biographer of Louis the Pious, the ninth-century emperor, claimed that his hero never "raised his voice in laughter when at festive times musicians, jesters, mimic actors, came to the feast in his presence." He adds that the pious one kept his teeth under cover even when "the people laughed with all their hearts." St. John Chrysostom had taught that Christ had never laughed. But the people did. Comedians and wandering minstrels plied their banquet entertainment. The hire of acrobats, mimes, and minstrels was included in lists of wedding expenses. Festivals and trade fairs were enlivened with acting as well as singing, dancing, juggling, acrobatics, puppet shows, and the antics of trained animals.

When a king or duke visited a city, a fuss was made. Special performances of religious plays were sometimes given and an amateur comedy troupe might prepare to

Fig. 2. *Student plays of the Middle Ages. These woodcuts were among forty-four illustrating the* Spiel von Kinderzucht *of Johann Rasser published in 1574. Rasser's school drama about how to raise children was performed outdoors in the summer of 1573 at Ensisheim near Colmar in Alsace. The open platform served for many scenes when set with a few props and when its curtain hangings were variously arranged. The audience sat on benches, stood, or observed from perches in trees or from house windows. Theatre Arts Prints.*

Fig. 3. *Stage erected for an entry, Antwerp, 1582. This is a showpiece that greeted the duke of Alençon, the youngest son of Henry II and Catherine de Medici, on his very elaborate entry into Antwerp in 1582. On the lower level, Discord was thrust into prison by Justice, an action necessary to the inauguration of a Golden Age. Theatre Arts Prints.*

entertain him. At times and in certain places professional players were engaged. Schoolboys would prepare to try the royal visitor's patience with their recitals. Royal entries featured well-wrought parades sometimes designed to impress the visitor and sometimes designed to impress the city. Often stages were erected in the streets. *Tableaux vivants* and allegorical shows proclaimed the virtues of the prince or the particular needs of his subjects, which he might supply if he were given some dramatic reminder of them. These shows can hardly be called plays. They were designed to present a congratulation or petition vividly and quickly. What prince compared in an entry display or tableau with Moses could fail to emulate the lawgiver in justice and wisdom, or fail to lift his countenance with a blander air when his deeds were set beside those of some heroic worthy on a stage set up in a city decked with tapestries, flags, garlands, greenery, and the scrubbed faces of a multitude in their Sunday best?

A man of the early sixteenth century inclined to speculate about the kind of plays a theatre should produce, about the manner of their performance and staging, would, in looking backward, have perceived the kind of theatre we have sketched above. In general, it was religious, the product of amateur effort, and confined to special festival occasions. Its plays had a diffuse structure that mixed moods and topics, and its stage presented a decorative assortment of mansions. The sixteenth-century change in the theatrical life of Europe, as we shall see, consisted of a rather sudden use of secular material, an increasing use of professional talent, an increasing frequency of perform-

FIG. 4. *Bas-Relief of a play, from the Farnese Palace, Rome. In this scene from a classic comedy, a drunken young man carries on to the accompaniment of a flute girl, and a slave attempts to quiet him. His irate father, counseled by an elderly companion, prepares a "warm" reception. Theatre Arts Prints.*

ance, and the use of a dramaturgy that had more unity and a stage that located the action in a unified scene.

We noted earlier the conservatism that marks theatrical activity. An individual may have his independent vision, but the army of collaborators needed to create a work of theatre art tends to find its vision in its own experience—in the past. When a change occurs, we must look somewhere outside the mainstream of the prevailing tradition to find the theatre artists, patrons, and audiences who will be needed if things are to be done differently. The courts of Italy during the Renaissance provided this necessary environment for change. There, the vision of a different theatre was first glimpsed by men who looked backward, far beyond the immediate past, beyond medieval forms, beyond the centuries of the Dark Ages, to a vision, the clearest they could bring into focus, of the theatre of the ancient world. As Italians, they looked to Rome.

NOTES

Émile Zola's complaint is quoted from p. 92 of *Papers on Playmaking,* edited by Brander Matthews, Hill and Wang, New York, 1957. The biographer of Louis the Pious is quoted from p. 251 of Eleanor Duckett's *Death and Life in the Tenth Century,* Ann Arbor, 1967.

Material in the chapter is given fuller treatment in Nicoll (*Development of the Theatre* and *Masks, Mimes and Miracles*), in Power, in Simonson (*The Stage Is Set*), in Kernodle, and in Southern. See bibliography for details of these publications.

Chapter II

THE COURT THEATRE AT FERRARA

What cared Duke Ercole, that bid
His mummers to the market-place,
What th' onion-sellers thought or did
So that his Plautus set the pace
For the Italian comedies.

—W. B. YEATS

Late in 1501 Don Alfonso d'Este, who four years later was to succeed his father, Ercole I, as duke of Ferrara, was married to Lucrezia Borgia. Donna Lucrezia, daughter of Pope Alexander VI, had an unsavory reputation fostered if not merited by a career that it might not be edifying to consider in detail. Let this suffice: her previous marriages, like this one to the house of Este, apparently had their beginning and end in the politics and power plays of that time. On the eve of this marriage, Duke Ercole's councillor wrote of Lucrezia's beauty and charm of manner, concluding, "We cannot and should not suspect her of unseemly behavior." And if the poets of that hour adorned her with virtues she may not have had, as was politic, for our part we might ignore the vices which some say she did have. After her last marriage, Lucrezia Borgia did not belie the poetic bouquets bestowed on her when it began; her later intimacies with a poet and a prince were probably Petrarchan. Her marriage dower brought to Ferrara 300,000 ducats, the reduction of the yearly tribute to Rome from 400,000 to a mere 100 ducats, plus certain fortresses and benefices. And at a time when the cities north of Romagna worried about where the Borgia would strike next, this

alliance gave Ferrara some assurance for the future.

The marriage was celebrated with dramatic doings in the two cities concerned. On December 23, 1501, the arrival of a Ferrarese escort at Rome was the first event in a two-week round of festivities in the papal city. Balls, comedies, allegorical shows, pageants, and dance pieces were part of the carnival surrounding the proxy marriage in the Vatican on December 30. There was also a bullfight which featured the bride's brother, Cesare Borgia, resplendent in gold braid. Cesare Borgia also devised an eclogue for a performance one evening. Duke Cesare's composition reflected the then-fashionable notion that, far from being bucolic louts, herdsmen were loquacious discussants of current events. Encouraged by Vergil's *Eclogae,* courtiers of the time embraced this fancy. Cesare's eclogue presented a setting of magnificent rusticity in which two shepherds chattered about the "shepherd of shepherds" (the Pope) protecting those on one side of a river (the Este) with the help of another on the other side (Cesare). In allegory, one thing is said and another is understood. A letter from Rome to Duke Ercole at home in Ferrara suggested to him that "he could count upon the aid of the Borgia against his enemies."

One evening, the *Menaechmi* of Plautus was played in the Pope's chamber. A dramatic allegory served as a prelude to the comedy and gilded the lily of this marriage. The dramatis personae included Virtue, Fortune, Glory, Caesar, Hercules, Juno, Rome, Jove, Ferrara, and Mercury, the messenger of the gods. The audience was more apt than we to translate these characters in terms that yielded the double meaning. Caesar was, of course, Cesare Borgia; Hercules, Duke Ercole d'Este; Jove, Alexander VI. Consider how gracious was the action of this piece. Glory in a triumphal car with the world beneath her feet ended the strife of Virtue and Fortune for precedence with the declaration that Caesar and Hercules had overcome Fortune by Virtue. The deeds of Cesare were related. Hercules conquered Fortune and released her on Juno's promise that neither Fortune nor Juno would ever oppose the houses of Este and Borgia. Rome in a chariot bewailed that Jove should deprive her of Lucrezia, "who was the refuge of all Rome." Ferrara gave assurance that Lucrezia was going to a worthy place and Mercury announced that the will of the gods was manifest in the arrangement. This substantial pageant faded with Mercury attending Ferrara in a triumphal chariot that passed in honor across the stage. After so much bother in the prologue, it is not surprising to learn that an actor in *Menaechmi* displayed his extempore wit by crying out when seized that he wondered how his captors could "use such violence to him, when Caesar and Hercules were on his side and Jove propitious." The improviser was applauded for his apt allusion.

On January 6, Lucrezia and her party set out from Rome and by the time of her state entry into Ferrara on February 2 she had received the honors of the towns en route. Courtesies spoke from stages set up at city gates and laudatious conceits displayed themselves in tableaux that arose before her. The shows at Foligno were typical. It does not need much imagination to know why at Foligno, Lucrezia of old Rome was declared surpassed in virtue by the living Lucrezia, nor to know why and how Paris judged again when he was presented in that capacity. One may pause, however, before the same city's spectacle of a sultan in a Turkish galley promising, for her sake, to restore Christian lands. Flattery attended Lucrezia's journey north.

The entry into Ferrara was heralded by the famous artillery pieces which were the special pride of Don Alfonso d'Este. Frightened by this blasting cannonade, Donna Lucrezia's horse threw her and so it was that a more docile mule bore the bride into the city. Her entry parade was as ostentatious as its final pack train of seventy mules which bore her dower and worldly goods into the city. Seventy-five archers in red and white led the big parade, and a group of eighty trumpeters in cloth of gold and purple and white satin marched behind. Twenty-four pipers and trumpeters marched before the nobles and gentlemen of Ferrara, seventy of those worthies adorned with gold chains. There was the suite of the duchess of Urbino in black velvet and satin. There was Don Alfonso in grey velvet covered with scales of beaten gold, and with him his brother-in-law, Messer Annibale Bentivoglio, the son of Bologna's ruler. There were eight squires in gold brocade and purple velvet, the bride's suite with twenty Spaniards in black and gold, followed by five bishops, ten ambassadors, six drummers, two Spanish jesters, the bride's horse, and eight grooms. There was the bride on her mule under a crimson canopy carried by doctors and escorted by six of the groom's chamberlains and the French ambassador. And there were the duchess of Urbino, the duke of Ferrara, three noble ladies, Madonna Lucrezia Bentivoglio, natu-

FIG. 5. *A torch dance, an engraving by Albrecht Dürer (1471–1528). Theatre Arts Prints.*

ral daughter of the duke of Ferrara, and the aforementioned seventy beasts of burden. Wending its conspicuous way into the city, this splendid parade passed triumphal arches with allegorical devices and mythological scenes. Four representations showed goddesses, Hercules (a favorite figure in a city whose reigning duke was Ercole), the god of love, nymphs, satyrs, and Europa mounted on the red bull of the house of Borgia. At the climactic entrance of Lucrezia into the piazza, acrobats performed. Two of them hurled themselves from two high towers and fell simultaneously at her feet. They were saved from disaster by "invisible" ropes. Prisoners were set free and festivities began which continued for the six days remaining before Lent. Carnival means farewell to the flesh, but not before appetites have had their days of indulgence.

For the plays which were the main feature of this celebration at Ferrara, Duke Ercole had erected a large shallow stage (it was about 10 feet deep and 80 feet wide) in a larger hall provided with amphitheatre seating. Over one hundred performers (men, women, and boys) and a like number of costumes were involved in the plays and dance interludes, as Duke Ercole made clear by having the performers' rich apparel

exhibited in a preview display. Thus was shown the magnanimity of the duke. All the plays were translations of Plautus (*Epidicus, Bacchides, Miles Gloriosus, Asinaria,* and *Casina*), and all were staged with dance interludes, or intermezzi. For example, *Miles Gloriosus* had between its five acts an intermezzo of men who danced with blazing torches, another of horned shepherds whose speciality was to butt one another as they danced, an intermezzo of the triumph of Cupid, and a rather exotic turn by jugglers of darts and daggers.

A source of information about the Ferrara celebration is a series of descriptive letters written by the groom's sister, Isabella d'Este. She did not enjoy it. Perhaps this *prima donna del mondo,* duchess of Mantua and quite conscious of her status as probably the most cultured girl of her time, could not have relished her subordinate role in a celebration that so emphatically hailed the Borgia princess. She wrote that the "few" arches erected for the entry parade had "some representations . . . not worth mentioning and no one paid much attention to them." She found the five hours devoted to *Bacchides* and its intermezzi tedious, and the Shrove Tuesday presentation of *Casina* seemed to her "lascivious and impure." One of the interludes that night was a dance featuring Don Alfonso and his brother Don Giulio, and in another a great globe was lowered on stage and Virtues came forth from it to praise Lucrezia. Isabella was not too impressed. Yet it is certain that Rome and Ferrara staged ambitious and spectacular celebrations and, particularly in Ferrara, theatricals dominated.

This theatrical festival was a herald of the kind then developing in the Renaissance courts of Italy and later in the courts of Europe. We look upon it as a fanfare for the revival of a secular theatre in Europe after the long quietus of medieval times. It seems the start of something different, but not all was new. This early sixteenth-century celebration had elements that were present in previous theatre activity. The processional elements were familiar forms, as were the personified abstractions, the allegorical shows, and the entry displays. But new elements seem to have been more numerous and obvious.

For one thing, the theatre had moved indoors, trading the sun for candles and the sky for a roof. It also had become an affair of state; princes and politicians presided, not priests or guild masters, and those presiding celebrated themselves and their doings, not the passions of scriptural heroes and prophets. They glorified themselves and their houses. The topic was their day and their affairs, however much they bandied classic myth to put a fine face on the matter. Allegorical figures of the kind now on stage were taken from pagan myth and the antique world. But these people were not suckling at a creed outworn; they were using these figures to talk about themselves in monologues that sounded the tune of their own glory.

Another new element was a more marked tendency toward professionalism. Because their theatre was so much a matter of their hour and that hour's business, these politicians had more need of professional theatre men than the medieval producers had. Last year's text, mansion, stage arrangement, spectacle device, and costume will not serve this season's embassy, marriage, entry, or reception. This was not a repetitive, nigh ritualistic, annual reenactment but the celebration of a unique event. Clever men were needed now to costume, erect the stage, arrange the lights, provide the scenery, translate, write the words of the allegorical dramas and the entry presentations, devise the intermezzi, and conceive the conceits that princes need to properly bestow and receive honor. Inventive stage

experts and writers were wanted for this work. The blatant flattery and the labored allusions of the allegories and the entry tableaux may not impress us as promising fields for artistic development. Yet these affairs gave occasion and opportunity to the professional. These opportunities would later enlarge and the amateur writing of Cesare Borgia's eclogue would be replaced.

At this date, some professionals were also needed to perform. Don Alfonso d'Este could grace a dance interlude and gentlemen, gentle ladies, and their apt children could act, dance, and appear prettily in pretty costume; but professionals are needed when acrobats must hurl themselves from towers, juggle daggers, and brandish firebrands. The mention of two Spanish jesters smacks of either slavery or professionalism. If not now, soon professional actors will be needed. As these political occasions elaborated their appropriate form of theatre, professional (full-time) experts became essential.

In addition to its political function and motive, and its inclination to bring in the professional, this theatre was also new in its concern with the learning and lore of the classic world. The audience was seated in a specially constructed amphitheatre at Ferrara because that was the way audiences sat at Rome more than a thousand years before. There were impersonations of classic gods and heroes and allusions to them and their stories. Plautus was the playwright. This theatre was colored by humanism, the characteristic intellectual movement of the Renaissance; by the light of humanism's concern for this day's life and that old world's literature, art, science, and philosophy; and by the nimbus of humanism's passion for learning. Here was a new kind of theatre. To see how it came to be and how it developed, we must take a closer backward look at Ferrara.

The theatre of Renaissance Italy was not

uniquely or even chiefly the work of Ferrarese artists, politicians, sycophants, and humanists; but Ferrara will serve best to illustrate the development of that theatre in the early years of the sixteenth century. We focus on Ferrara because at that time it was the center of an unusual amount of varied activity. Although it had then a population of 100,000, almost twice that of Rome, and although it was a much wealthier city than its subsequent history would lead us to suppose, it is to the credit of the Este dukes that Ferrara had a century and a half of distinction. When Machiavelli needed an example of a successful hereditary principate, he chose the duke of Ferrara. In an Italy where governments were not stable, the Estensi maintained a political regime that, if not ideal, could in some way be depended upon. And their interest in dramatic entertainments of varied kinds could be depended upon as well. Duke Ercole was a parsimonious man but a generous patron of his theatre. This was not so clearly the case in other Italian cities, where ruler could be depended upon to succeed or usurp ruler but not necessarily to continue any policy of patronage of drama and theatre.

The Estensi's sustaining interest in theatre was not matched in any other European city in the early years of the sixteenth century. This interest can be traced to the early fifteenth century. Niccolo d'Este, the third of that name to rule in Ferrara, enjoyed the pleasures of an exuberant character and a long reign in a city where his family had effectually ruled for a hundred years before him. Niccolo III enjoyed the boast, if not the certain knowledge, that he had had more than 800 women for his pleasure. And when he died in 1441 there reigned after him his heirs: Leonello, Borso, and Ercole. The Estensi were to maintain their power throughout the sixteenth century, the generations succeeding Niccolo down to Alfonso II, the last Este duke, whom we may glimpse in the lurid light of Browning's dramatic lyric, "My Last Duchess," as he mutters of his "nine-hundred-year-old name" and of his choosing "never to stoop."

The earlier fifteenth-century rulers—Niccolo, Leonello, and Borso—sponsored the study and created the atmosphere that led to the more theatrically notable reign of Ercole I, the period from 1471 to 1505. The rediscovery of ancient learning and an enthusiasm for it, a sine qua non of the Renaissance, had been a feature of life at the Este court. In 1429, Niccolo brought to Ferrara a noted humanist and brilliant scholar named Guarini as a teacher for his sons. For his teacher's sake, Leonello secured one of the first manuscripts of Plautus' comedies, including twelve plays supposedly lost that had come to light the year before. The library at Ferrara became outstanding. So did the circle that gathered about Leonello, the avid scholar-prince. When Leonello issued a decree for the reformation of the university, he expressed the attitude of the true Renaissance humanist: the earth must some day perish—Rome herself lies in the dust—but the understanding of things we call wisdom is not extinguished by length of years. The revival of learning in Italy at this time meant among other things a revival of interest in Latin comedy and tragedy which was evidenced by the composition of derivative, imitative, rather unattractive pieces in Latin that today are celebrated by pedants. They are literary rather than dramatic pieces, exercises in rhetoric to be read rather than performed. Two early examples of humanist tragedy in Latin were composed at Ferrara. Francesco Ariosti's *Isis* was recited before Leonello and his court, and Laudivio's *De captivitate ducis jacobi* was prepared for a reading at the palace during the reign of Borso.

This was the background, an indication

FIG. 6. *Actors and audience for a comedy. From a 1497 edition of Terence published at Venice. Theatre Arts Prints.*

of preparation, but not a movement toward a lively form of theatre. The medieval religious drama had by this time embraced the vernacular, but this humanist circle was drawn to its library, where the language was Latin and where its fancy was engaged by visions of old Rome. Its plays were recited in Latin to a congenial audience quite comfortable and delighted with echoes of Seneca. The blessings of this humanism were not spread far beyond rather small cultivated circles, nor were they displayed to any theatre public.

Yet, in Ferrara on January 25, 1486, on the occasion of a visit by Isabella d'Este's intended, the marquis of Mantua, Duke Ercole unveiled before his people a production of Plautus' *Menaechmi.* The date has been labeled the birthday of the modern Italian drama because it marked a new di-

rection. This was no exercise in closet studiousness but an open-air performance before a huge crowd (one writer says 10,000 attended). The play was acted, not read, it was staged in a new way, and what is more, it was translated from Latin to the vernacular. Battista Guarini, son of the humanist teacher who had come to Ferrara a half-century before, was the translator. It was the first recorded production of its kind in Europe. *Menaechmi* was staged in the palace courtyard and acted in front of a setting of five houses. It featured an impressive boat outfitted with oars and sails that could carry ten people across the courtyard. The audience was accommodated in an amphitheatre. There was a fireworks display after the show.

The next year, 1487, Ferrara's position as a leading contributor to the developing Italian Renaissance theatre was enhanced. In the same courtyard where *Menaechmi* was performed, another setting of a city was erected and this time *"una cosa mirabile da vedere,"* a medieval paradise with children as the seven planets (not, be it noted, as circling angels), loomed over the houses on one side of the stage. And so was staged Plautus' *Amphitruo,* the naughty tale of how Jupiter tricked Alcmena to beget Hercules, and at the end Jupiter, rather than a saint or our blessed savior, was assumpted on high. There were two performances of the naughty comedy. The first, given on January 25 to celebrate the marriage of Ercole's natural daughter Lucrezia, was interrupted by rain. The second, performed on February 3 with the marquis of Mantua attending, was not rained out, and Hercules, whose namesake presided at the performances, appeared in a pageant of his labors provided as an afterpiece. In this same carnival season of 1487, Duke Ercole honored the marriage of a favorite courtier by presenting an original Italian play written by Niccola da Correggio. This was *Fa-*

vola di Cefalo, one of the first Italian non-religious plays to be performed.

Other plays of Plautus were translated and performed in Ferrara in the final years of Duke Ercole's reign. New plays also were written. There was a steady diet of Plautine comedy, especially the most popular one of all, *Menaechmi,* which was performed on at least five occasions. When Lucrezia Borgia came to Ferrara at the beginning of the new century, she entered a city that was probably better able than any other to provide a five-day festival of Roman comedy.

These revivals of Roman comedy did not suddenly supplant the earlier religious pieces. The two existed side by side at Ferrara and each had its season. Duke Ercole took equal pride in his humanist courtiers and in Ferrara's holy nun who had received the stigmata. The Feast of Corpus Christi continued to be celebrated with a solemn procession. There is an account of how the Passion of Christ was represented in the *duomo* on Good Friday, 1503. A mansion of Calvary was placed before the high altar, another provided a hell-mouth gaping to embrace choristers robed as the fathers in Limbo, and, aloft, a heaven opened for an angel's descent. After Easter that year at the house of the archbishop, the Annunciation, the Visitation of St. Elizabeth, and the Dream of Joseph were performed. Isabella d'Este described the last play thus: "The heavens opened again . . . to manifest the Incarnation of Jesus to Joseph, and to set his doubts at rest regarding the Conception of the Holy Virgin." The Annunciation presented the angel Gabriel, and Isabella wrote an enthusiastic description of the effective stagecraft:

Then Mary appeared, under a portico supported by eight pillars and began to repeat some verses from the Prophets, and while she spoke, the sky opened, revealing a figure of God the Father, surrounded by a choir of angels. No support could be seen either for His feet or for those of the angels, and six other seraphs hovered in the air, suspended by chains. In the center of the group was the Archangel Gabriel, to whom God the Father addressed His word, and after receiving his orders, Gabriel descended with admirable artifice and stood, half-way in the air, at the same height as the organ. Then all of a sudden, an infinite number of lights broke out at the foot of the angel choir, and hid them in a blaze of glory. . . . At that moment the Angel Gabriel alighted on the ground, and the iron chain which he held was not seen, so that he seemed to float down on a cloud. . . .

We wonder if the techniques of this traditional medieval stagecraft were used when comedies were staged in the duke's courtyard and great hall. Did Mercury descend with the same admirable artifice as Gabriel? The outdoor 1486 *Menaechmi* with its five houses may suggest that Plautus was simply placed on a medieval mansion stage. The boat that crossed the courtyard is reminiscent of the ship on the Sea of Galilee at Valenciennes. But it may be more accurate to see this setting as a new type, to see a unified picture, to see a "classical" street scene with five houses on the street rather than five separate houses or mansions. We are tempted to see it this way because of what was done later and because we know that the *Menaechmi* setting was the work of Pellegrino Prisciani, a Ferrarese humanist who had studied the Roman architect Vitruvius in manuscript and had digested the writings and comments of the scholar-architect Alberti. Moreover, Prisciani wrote an illustrated archaeological pamphlet based partly on his own observations of classic remains. From this we know that his conception of staging was consonant with that of later Renaissance architects. Scenery came to be not an accumulation of separate things but a unity with the parts organized as a whole. Prisciani conceived not of a multiple or simultaneous setting but of an acting platform placed in front of a unified scenic background. If not a Roman theatre, this was a Renaissance architect's conception of a Roman theatre. Humanism came in the stage door with the designer.

In addition to the unified picture, Italian painter-architects added another element to staging: perspective. According to Vasari, Brunelleschi "gave considerable attention to the study of perspective," and so did many others. Of the artists who studied and mastered perspective, none provides so piquant an anecdote as Paolo Uccelo. When he was entreated by his wife to sleep rather than spend the night "seeking new expressions of his rules of perspective," he replied with the exclamation, "Oh what a delightful thing is this perspective!" Uccelo was typical of the fifteenth-century artists who happily worked to perfect this means of presenting depth on a flat surface. This kind of perspective, using lines that advanced in depth to a central vanishing point, does not excite our wonder. But in that day it was new and brightly fascinating. It was a key to a mysterious kind of mastery; it was logical, harmonious, calculable, exciting. Painter and connoisseur cried with Uccelo, "Oh what a delightful thing!"

There is a scant account of productions of *Amphitruo* and *Menaechmi* at Ferrara in 1491 and of Niccolò del Cogo providing the stage with a "prospect of four castles." What did "prospect" mean? A letter describing the plays presented during carnival at Ferrara in 1508 is a more certain record of this "delightful thing" on stage. The writer was definite:

> But what has been best in all these festivities and representations has been the scenery . . . which Master Peregrino (Pellegrino da Udine at Ferrara, 1502–13) the Duke's painter has made. It has been a view in perspective of a town with houses, churches, belfries and gardens, such that one could never tire of looking at it, because of the different things that are there, all most cleverly designed and executed. I suppose that this will not be destroyed, but that they will preserve it to use on other occasions.

By the use of perspective, the artist brought to the scenic background the architectural features of a crowded town. Surely, the writer supposes, this kind of setting was not for one season. This, the "best of all," would be kept, for "one could never tire of looking at it." Although we cannot be sure a perspective setting was first used at Ferrara in 1508 (scenic backgrounds of the type appeared at many Italian courts in the early years of the century), this letter is our first record of such a setting.

In the history of the Ferrarese stage, the year 1508 was notable for another reason, as the same letter records:

> On Monday evening the Cardinal (Ippolito d'Este, brother of Duke Alfonso) had a comedy performed, which was composed by Messer Lodovico Ariosto, his familiar, and rendered in the form of a farce or merry jape, the which from the beginning to end was as elegant and as delightful as any other that I have ever seen played, and it was much commended on every side. The subject was a most beautiful one of two youths enamoured of two harlots . . . there were so many intrigues and novel incidents and so many fine moralities and various things that in those of Terence there are not half of them.

The new and good playwright was Ariosto, his comedy was *Cassaria,* and although it was an imitation of Roman comedy, it was also the first fully developed Italian play. "I present you a new comedy," declared the author in his prologue, which then sounded an apology for braving the time's fashion and taste. "I seem to see the majority inclined to blame it, as soon as I have said *new* . . . they only deem what the ancients have composed to be perfect." We may suppose either that Ariosto contrived better than he knew or that his audience, after so long an exposure to the ancients in translation, was inclined another way. At any rate, the next year Lodovico Ariosto's "much commended" comedy was followed by another success, his best-known play, *Suppositi*. It impressed its audience as "an entirely modern comedy." It interests us even more than *Cassaria,* for its characters and setting present the Ferrara of the poet's student days.

Lodovico Ariosto's association with the theatre had begun during the reign of Duke Ercole. He may have seen the 1486 production of *Menaechmi* when he was 12. Two years later, when Ariosto was a law student, he probably saw the court productions and may have acted in them, as students and the sons of noblemen were wont to do. At least it was so in the summer of 1493, when four Roman comedies were performed at Pavia by a company of twenty youths that included Ariosto. These comedians were brought to Pavia by Duke Ercole on a state visit to Lodovico il Moro, duke of Milan, husband of Ercole's daughter Beatrice. In 1503 Ariosto entered the service of Cardinal Ippolito d'Este. For a quarter-century afterwards, except for the presentations of the comedies mentioned above, he was not often at Ferrara nor much engaged in theatrics, but traveling throughout Italy on diplomatic-political missions for the cardinal. During this time, Ariosto wrote the first edition of his romantic epic, *Orlando Furioso,* which was brought out in 1516. At Ferrara, theatre activity was virtually suspended as Duke Alfonso engaged his energies and those of his people in the tussles, tensions, and terrors of a period of war. Those years present a tangled tale. How tangled is at the heart of a story about the duke encouraging his cannoneers to fire away at the bat-

tle of Ravenna with these words: "You cannot make a mistake; they are all our enemies." Perhaps we may also avoid discriminating between friend and foe. Ariosto entered the service of Duke Alfonso in 1518.

There was a production of Ariosto's *Suppositi* at Rome in 1519. The Pontiff of the time was Leo X, who had provided his own portrait when he breathed the indiscreet exhortation, "Let us enjoy the papacy since God has given it to us." Leo enjoyed the decor provided by the great Raphael for this production of *Suppositi*. A Ferrarese in attendance wrote to Duke Alfonso that it was "not given with the perfection with which I have seen such things presented in your Lordship's hall." Perhaps Ferrara did this sort of thing better than Rome—they had had more practice. But we could hardly expect his Lordship's hall to compare poorly to the Pope's in his Lordship's mail.

Raphael had made a perspective scene of Ferrara. There the *Suppositi* was supposed to be and there we might expect the scene to convey us, except in that time the setting did not usually correspond so nicely with the play. We wonder if Ferrara enjoyed so piquant a touch when the play was done there ten years before. It was usual for the same street scene setting to serve an entire carnival series of plays. And in 1509, when this comedy was first performed, it was linked with comedies by Terence. Would Terence have been presented with an obviously Ferrarese setting displayed behind the actors? Or would Ariosto, who translated the Terence plays performed that year, have gone a bit further and adapted them to home town?

Ariosto returned to Ferrara and active work in the court theatre in 1528. That year the future Duke Ercole II (son of Duke Alfonso and Lucrezia Borgia d'Este) married Renée of France. For the entry of the royal couple in December, Alfonso's artillery reverberated as they had for the entry of his own bride in 1502. Again they heralded a series of plays. There was a French translation of the ever popular *Menaechmi* provided with Italian explanatory verses before each act by Ariosto. Two of the poet's comedies were also performed. Besides a new verse version of *Cassaria,* there was the first performance of Ariosto's *La Lena,* a study of low life in Ferrara.

The winter of 1528–29 brought the inauguration of what may have been the first permanent theatre built in Europe in the thousand years since Roman times. It was set up in the court above a loggia, overlooking the piazza. The theatre was erected under the direction of Ariosto with magnificent scenery painted by Ferrara's greatest artist, Dosso Dossi. Unlike the usual stage, built anew each season when plays were to be performed, this stage was to serve from year to year. Nor was this merely a matter of lumber and architecture. The new theatre was animated by a permanent director when Ariosto became, in effect, its supervisor. He served four years in this capacity, having a main hand in productions of final versions of his *Cassaria, Lena,* and *Negromante,* as well as in productions of Plautus and Terence.

On at least two occasions during this time, Angelo Beolco, an extraordinary Paduan, appeared at the Ferrarese court as an entertainer. Beolco is one of the earliest professional actors about whose career we have any knowledge. He was active for some twenty years after 1520, when he began appearing as Ruzzante, a humorous fellow from the Paduan countryside. Beolco was the author of monologues and comedies that blended neoclassic elements with rustic farce and the humor of regional types. As an author Beolco preferred a style based on careful observation of the speech of simple folk, and as the actor of

Ruzzante he developed his art along similar lines. He had a small company that was not regularly organized but was prepared when the opportunity arose to perform at carnival time. It was with such a group that Beolco appeared at Ferrara in the 1529 celebration of Don Ercole's wedding, "singing and disputing" at a banquet given after the performance of *Cassaria.* In 1532 Beolco wrote his patron about another performance at Ferrara for which he was bringing fine costumes. He wrote he would not arrive in time to supervise the construction of the setting, but he expressed confidence that Ariosto would take care of that detail. Because Beolco was in some sense an improviser (as are all entertainers) and because he appeared in the "mask" of Ruzzante, he is sometimes considered the first recorded performer of commedia dell'arte. He illustrates the entry of professional acting into the court theatre.

Unhappily, on the last day of the year 1532, a tremendous fire consumed Ariosto's theatre at Ferrara. Its luster of permanence vanished after four short years. Sorrow at the sight of so much ruined magnificence supposedly helped bring on the

FIG. 7. *Design for the "Comic Scene," Serlio, 1545. Theatre Arts Prints.*

poet's death early in the summer of 1533. A writer of the time linked the fire and the day of Ariosto's death in a cosmic scheme: "The burning of that scene was a sign in anticipation of his death even as a comet or thunder bolt presages the death of princes." No recorded comet or thunderbolt announced the death of the doughty cannoneer Duke Alfonso a year after, when Ferrara's ruler died apparently not so much in sorrow as from eating too much melon. So passed a theatre, a poet, a prince, and a brief period in the history of the stage.

As it was at Ferrara, so in some ways it was at other Italian courts of the period. From a humanist interest in Latin plays and Roman theatre practice, the court at Ferrara had moved to productions of plays in translation, mounted on a stage that was an attempt at a reconstruction of the Roman model. A little later appeared Ariosto's comedies based on the models of classic comedy yet modern in setting, mood, and character. From the setting of *Menaechmi* in 1486 on a temporary outdoor stage was developed the perspective scene of the permanent theatre erected and used four decades later in 1528. Professional theatre artists appeared—first translators, writers, and stage designers and then performers. From a humanistic, scholarly concern with classic theatre there developed a theatre art at the service of the dukes, celebrating their acts and enhancing their glory.

NOTES

The headnote is taken from Yeats' poem "To a Wealthy Man Who Promised a Second Subscription To The Dublin Municipal Gallery If It were Proved The People Wanted Pictures." These lines are reprinted with permission of Macmillan Publishing Co., Inc., from *The Collected Poems of W. B. Yeats,* by W. B. Yeats, copyright 1916 by Macmillan Publishing Co., Inc., renewed 1944 by Bertha Georgie Yeats.

"We cannot . . . suspect her" appears on p. 219 of Bellonci; "he could count upon the aid . . ." is on p. 410 of Gardner's *Dukes and Poets,* where the account of the Rome *Menaechmi* also is given; Isabella's objections to the entry displays are in Cartwright's biography, p. 205; her objection to *Casina* appears on p. 420 of Gardner's book; the courtyard setting marvelous to behold quote is from Beijer's article; Isabella's description of the Dream of Joseph and the Annunciation is from *Isabella d'Este,* Vol. 1, by Julia Cartwright, published in 1903 by E. P. Dutton & Co. Inc., and used with their permission; the story of Uccelo's fascination with perspective is given on the first page of Simonson's *The Art of Scenic Design;* "prospect of four castles" is on p. 82 of Nicoll's *Development;* Gardner's *The King of Court Poets* (p. 323) provides the description of the 1508 production of *Cassaria*—Constable and Co. have given permission to quote from it; in the same book is Ariosto's prologue (p. 324) and the account of *Suppositi* (p. 326); Alfonso's battle cry at Ravenna is given by Gilbert (p. 59); the letter about *Suppositi* at Rome is quoted in Gardner's *The King of Court Poets* (p. 330); Beolco's "singing and disputing" appears in Lea (p. 252); Gardner's *The King of Court Poets* tells of the "burning of that scene" on p. 259. See the bibliography for details of these books.

In preparing this chapter, the Beijer article and the works of Bellonci, Cartwright, Gardner, Herrick, and Noyes were especially valuable.

Chapter III

SIXTEENTH-CENTURY PLAYS AND CRITICISM

*If we present a Tragedy, we include the fatal
and abortive ends of such as commit notorious
murders . . . to terrify men from the like ab-
horred practices. . . . If a comedy . . . to
show others their slovenly and unhandsome behavior, that they may reform.*

—THOMAS HEYWOOD

A brief account of the plays of the Italian Renaissance theatre begins with a notice of Angelo Poliziano's *Favola d'Orfeo,* which was produced at the Gonzaga court in Mantua, dated variously from 1471 to 1480. The medieval structure of its plot is noted as well as its design for performance on a multiple setting. For this dramatization of the Orpheus and Eurydice story there were pastoral locales and the gates of Hades as well as that place itself. *Orfeo* ranks as the first Italian play of the new era because, although its structure was old and designed for an "old" method of staging, its subject was new and reflected a humanist interest in classic lore. There were elements in it (nymphs and shepherds and songs) that foretell the development of the later pastoral play and opera. We have mentioned a similar play staged at Ferrara in 1487—the next Italian play to be performed after *Orfeo,* Correggio's *Favola di Cefalo.* We might expect that Poliziano's sort of play would appear, that there might have been in many plays a marriage of secular, classic matter with medieval manner. Despite expectation, this was not the usual practice. In libraries and in academic courtly circles, the superior form of Roman drama dazzled all who perceived it and a host of assiduous apes harked after Thalia and Melpomene in that direction.

The language itself had something to do with this fascination for Roman drama. Latin was the language of school, learning, and church, and it was international. By the late fourteenth century, Italian had been enhanced by the work of Dante, Petrarch, and Boccaccio, but the Italians (Petrarch among them) thought that any literature worthy the name must be in Latin. There was a similar attitude about theatre; dramas of any pretension must be Latin dramas. Terence had been read throughout the medieval period; now Plautus and Seneca were studied as well. New plays for a new era, if humanist taste had anything to do with it, would be Latin, not only in language but also in structure, topic, and tone.

The earliest surviving humanist Latin tragedy, *Eccerinis,* was written for reading before a Paduan circle by Albertino Mussato. A historical tragedy imitative of Seneca, *Eccerinis* dates from the early fourteenth century. Other Senecan Latin plays are noted by literary historians. Though

31

many were not performed, they are evidence that the humanists and their sixteenth-century descendants were uniquely receptive to Seneca's peculiar quality. The works of the first-century Roman (whose own plays may not have been more than closet drama designed for reading rather than performance) became imposing models. Early in the sixteenth century, Greek tragedy became available in print and had some effect on playwriting but not enough to displace Seneca's stronger influence. His blend of horror, sententious stoicism, and thrilling rhetoric gave off a dramatic glow that was well liked. How to construct a plot, how to begin a play near the climax in order to concentrate an effect, was learned from Seneca, but with that gain in knowledge came a fierce dealing in terrific melodrama. Also came Furies, ghosts, messengers, and revenge.

The appropriate example of Seneca's plays is *Thyestes,* which may be rudely summarized as follows. In Act One a Fury goads the ghost of Tantalus with a recital of the crimes of his house. Murder, incest, adultery, excessive ambition, and lust are in the list. Thyestes (a son of this distinguished house) had sought to usurp the kingdom from his brother Atreus, had seduced his brother's wife, and had been exiled. In Act Two Atreus, determined on revenge, plans to lure Thyestes home. In Act Three Thyestes returns. If this act created any expectation of brotherly dealing by Atreus, the next act is a thrilling reversal. In Act Four a messenger reports the revenge. In Act Five Thyestes is shown feasting on the flesh of his children at a banquet prepared by the revenging Atreus. The heads of the children are then displayed on a special platter brought before the agonized Thyestes.

This play was relished. If weighed on a scale that balances imitations, *Thyestes* was

as popular as *Menaechmi,* the former as esteemed a tragedy as the latter a comedy. Versions of Seneca, Greek tragedy, and stories from Ovid and Roman history were done and redone. With few exceptions they all had a Senecan mood and mold, some excessively so. For example, an early fifteenth-century *Progne* featured a heroine whose husband raped her sister and cut out the ravished one's tongue. This did not prevent the heroine from learning of the crime, and her revenge consisted of serving the husband their son in stew dish and roast platter. The victim's head was brought before the appalled husband by his mutilated, mute, and aforetime ravished sister-in-law. *Progne* was not performed.

School exercises provided the first stagings of comedy and tragedy. Academic revivals of Roman plays gave scholars and elite audiences intimations of classic grandeur as schoolboys in Italy and Europe strutted in the language. Case endings rang in the ears of the gods again. At the Roman Academy, Julius Pomponius Laetus (a Latin name) led these stagings with a series of revivals staged during the latter part of the fifteenth century. Patronized and applauded by leaders of the church and cultivated society, these performances were given on special occasions. Such an occasion was the visit of Eleanora of Aragon to Rome on her way to Ferrara after her marriage to Duke Ercole d'Este in 1473. A series of Latin plays was given at great expense. Similar revivals were staged later in other Italian cities and as far away as England, where king and cardinal and their distinguished guests basked in the reflected glory of such entertainments in London early in the sixteenth century. Soon original, if closely imitative, vernacular plays were to take stage.

The first to be performed were comedies. In addition to Ariosto, and closely

FIG. 8. *A scenic design of Baldassare Peruzzi. This is probably a design for* Calandria, *as produced at Rome in 1514. The scene is composed of angle wings on each side of the stage with a flat backdrop upstage of them. The actors may have played within the area defined by the first two houses, for there does not seem to be much of an acting platform in front. From* The Theatre *by Sheldon Cheney, published by David McKay Company, Inc.*

rivaling him in popularity, was Bernardo Dovizio da (later Cardinal) Bibbiena, whose *Calandria* was first staged at Urbino in 1513. A reworking of the *Menaechmi* jape of mistaken identity, *Calandria* presented as an extra flllip a twin brother and sister who dressed in the garb of the opposite sex. Pietro Aretino exploited the same naughty device when he wrote *Talanta,* another *Menaechmi*-inspired concoction that complicated complexity by using triplets.

(Shakespeare's later version, *The Comedy of Errors,* used two sets of twins, masters and servants, as did a commedia dell'arte scenario of the same later time.) Aretino's comedies were sharply satiric. Probably the best comedy of this time was written by Niccolò Machiavelli. His *Mandragola* has been revived today, although it seems to have been seldom produced then. If these few comedies by Ariosto, Dovizio, Machiavelli, and Aretino were all that had popularity or distinction, they were at least the best written in Italian before Goldoni. They are valued more than the tragedies in Italian which appeared onstage a little later in the century.

The first Italian tragedy formed in the classic mold that was successfully staged was Giambattista Giraldi Cinthio's *Orbecche*. Cinthio dramatized one of his own *novelle* for performance at his home in Ferrara, where it appeared in 1541. The court and Cinthio's patron, Duke Ercole II, were in attendance. It was a success, not only pleasing a court more used to comedy but also giving tragic performances a vogue they had not had before in Italy—exactly what Cinthio had hoped. Nine printings of *Orbecche* appeared in the fifty years after its premiere; its author enjoyed a reputation as the best of tragic poets and the flattery of imitations.

Act One of *Orbecche* does not have much to do with the subsequent action, but it is faithful to Seneca in its fashioning and it does foreshadow and produce a mood. Nemesis asks the Furies to take vengeance on the Persian tyrant Sulmone and his daughter Orbecche. The ghost of Selina, Sulmone's wife, whom he killed years ago, appears for vengeance also. Sulmone had killed her when their daughter had in some unwitting way revealed that Selina and her son were guilty of incest. This kind of carrying-on in the nether regions was *the* way to begin a tragedy. So had begun *Thyestes* and earlier plays; so would begin many later plays. Of course, Hamlet's father's ghost appears on the battlements, but he comes mantled in the same Stygian gloom of "shapes and shrieks, and sights unholy!" Earthbound in Act Two, Cinthio's play has Orbecche make some revelations to her nurse. Sulmone would marry Orbecche to the king of Parthia, but Orbecche is secretly married to Oronte and they have two sons. Sulmone's anger is

anticipated. In Act Three Malecche, a sage counselor, pleads with Sulmone to forgive his daughter Orbecche and her no longer secret husband, Oronte. Sulmone apparently relents. In Act Four a messenger (who had similarly served in the same act in *Thyestes*) reports horrors: Sulmone has butchered Oronte and his sons. In Act Five Sulmone sets a banquet. The meat is, of course, suspect, although not immediately to the heroine. Not until Orbecche is about to feast on husband and sons does she discover the butcher's knife in one of the platters. Drawing the knife from its fleshy sheath, she mortally wounds Sulmone, who expires offstage. Orbecche returns with the tyrant's head in her hands and imprecations on her lips. Orbecche's suicide ends this strange, eventful history.

Orbecche supposedly inspired the Paduan litterateur Sperone Speroni to attempt a surpassing tragedy. This was *Canace* and it dramatized an incestuous union, the killing of the child of that union, the suicides of the partners, and some smack of repentance.

A summarizing statement from Scaliger's *Poetics* of 1561 may be offered in lieu of a multiplication of examples or further mention of the tragic poets of the era. "The matters of tragedy are great and terrible, as commands of kings, slaughters, despairs, suicides, exiles, bereavements, parricides, incests, conflagrations, battles, the putting out of eyes, weeping, wailing, bewailing, eulogies, and dirges." Great and terrible as they were, there is more to Seneca and to Cinthio than bald, brief accounts of their plays' action suggests. No play written for the stage can be judged on the page, and the best of tragedies can be turned to farce if cut drastically. If these slapdash sketches of *Thyestes, Progne, Orbecche,* and *Canace* are unjust in their descriptions of the action of the pieces, they are as unjust in their silence about the sentiment. We may adjust our impression by considering Cinthio's explanation of why he preferred Senecan tragedy to Greek. Seneca, he wrote, "surpasses in prudence, in gravity, in decorum, in majesty, in sentiments all the Greeks who ever wrote, although in style he could have been more correct than he is." The comment is startling in its unexpectedness and it advises us that the times beheld more in these plays than grisly events dwelt on. On the other hand, these events *were* dwelt on to the apparent delight of their audiences and to the disgust of later critics. These playwrights seem to croak a ghastly promise to their audience: "Now I will horrify you."

During the latter years of the sixteenth century appeared some influential criticism based on the *Poetics* of Aristotle and the writings of Horace, so far as they were understood. Standards of correctness developed that were shaped by Seneca's practice and by that of the tragic poets of the time. Italians such as Antonio Sebastiano Minturno, Julius Caesar Scaliger, and Lodovico Castelvetro expounded theories about the need to separate tragedy and comedy, about the importance of rhetorical and didactic elements, about the five-act form and about the so-called three unities of time, place, and action. For a long time after, the unities seemed important matters of rule. Nowadays, most theorists would agree that only thematic unity is of moment, and some venturers have wondered about that. When they meet in heaven (if that is where critics go), these heretics will be able to argue the matter with their Renaissance counterparts. The latter conceived of drama as a literary art, which of course it is not. Their conception of theatre could hardly have been much larger than they could gather from reading. Given the paucity of productions and the comparatively abundant supply of texts, we should not be surprised. These critics, when read today, amuse by their wrong-headedness and yet are instructive in the light their notions shed on the plays of their time and for two centuries after.

We may taste the quality of this criticism in Castelvetro's argument that "the scene of the action must be constant, being not merely restricted to one city or house, but indeed to that one place alone which could be visible to one person." This is logical. Yet carried to its logical conclusion, it approaches the ridiculousness of Castelvetro's argument for limiting the time of action to twelve hours. "There is no possibility of making the spectators believe that many days and nights have passed, when they themselves obviously know that only a few hours have actually elapsed; they refuse to be so deceived." Think of that. We hear it echoed in Coleridge's phrase about "the willing suspension of disbelief," also nonsense when one thinks of it carefully. One wonders what undeceived audiences Castelvetro had ever been with. How mulish of them not to be deceived! How wicked of him to wish to deceive them! Ah, but it was a time for rules. It has been estimated that in the sixteenth century there were 200 editions and commentaries on Aristotle. Against the tide, Aretino might declare, "The best teacher is actual performance, which, repeated frequently, leads to knowledge. The inventive mind learns more this way than from other people." The apothegm, "It is better to drink from one's own wooden cup than out of someone else's golden chalice," did not seem true. The critical writings of this period had their subsequent effect on European drama, particularly French neoclassic tragedy, and fine brains were addled by the problem posed: how to make practice conform to rule.

In terms of dramatic literature, the period under review produced a few comedies, no tragedies that interest us today, and some influential dramatic criticism.

Why did this theatre, so splendid in some respects, fail to produce great drama? Several answers have been given. One suggests that because this theatre cultivated showy scenic display, it could not also be a theatre of great plays. "But what has been best . . . has been the scenery," wrote the man who saw Ariosto's first comedy. It may have been so. Ben Jonson was later to write of poetry and picture that they are "arts of a like nature, and both are busy about imitation." This statement sounds fair enough except for poetry, for we know busy pictures are busier—they take the eye—and when there is much to look at in the theatre, there is not much that is listened to. We speak of "seeing" a play, yet dramatic poetry comes in the ear, as the Elizabethans knew for they spoke of going to "hear" a play. A theatre of spectacle is seldom a theatre of literary distinction. And then there is the matter of this theatre's raison d'être. Its princely patrons wanted matter for carnival and celebration, something for politic eyes. No dramatic poet's dialogue of what is and what might be could be preferred to an affirming monologue of what the bill-paying prince wanted others to think of him. The prologue, intermezzo, or pageant after the play where this could be shown was, therefore, more important. In the early *Favola d'Orfeo* there was a song, sung by no less a personage than Orpheus himself, in praise of a Mantuan cardinal.

Part of the answer to the question of the paucity of first-class plays may be given by those who have deplored that the writing was so uniformly and carefully modeled to classic examples and that in tragedy Seneca, rather than the Greeks, was esteemed as the supreme example. Although masterpieces have been based on earlier plays and originality in story and construction may not be as important as we today are apt to believe it is, the imitations of this period seem to have been unpromisingly slavish.

A less reverent treatment of this same classic comic material has created some of our theatre's greatest bits. Giraudoux has given us a sophisticated Plautus with *Amphitryon 38,* its very title suggesting how unoriginal his material was. And *A Funny Thing Happened on the Way to the Forum* made superb use of Plautus.

Another suggestion is that academic standards and critical rules dominated the work being done. Lope de Vega, the great Spanish dramatist, described his method of writing comedy as being preceded by an almost ritualistic exorcism of Roman models. "I lock in the precepts with six keys, I banish Terence and Plautus from my study . . . and I write in accordance with that art which they devised who aspired to the applause of the crowd." As an anonymous poet put it, "Handsome is as handsome does." The critics and lovers of theory are not to be scorned; nor are they to be adored. Does poetry derive from rule, or does rule derive from poetry? Perhaps playwrights should not too ardently aspire to the applause of the crowd, yet all great dramas have won that applause. To an unhappy degree, these plays were for a limited circle and not for the crowd at all. Perhaps the models and rules were too restrictive and perhaps the clientele was as finicky as its exclusiveness suggests.

Probably an overriding reason for the failure to produce great dramas was the disruptive political instability of Italy. It was difficult for a prince to establish his seat in a city and take his ease, much less for any Italian city to give a theatre company a permanent home. Ferrara came closest, but even there no opportunity arose for a steady, year-in, year-out development. The theatre is a communal art and the part-time devotion of a community to that art, no matter how suddenly lavish, cannot accomplish what a more modest, steady nurture can. There was talent in Italy. but it

Fig. 9. *Design by Herman Rosse for a modern revival of* Mandragola. *Theatre Arts Prints.*

was mobilized only occasionally when it could serve the need or pleasure of a prince, and so it could not develop professionally. Playwrights are made, in part, by the theatre they serve. In an intermittent theatre, they serve in part. The master dramatists, Shakespeare and Molière, were both involved in a workaday theatre, were both deeply committed to their theatre companies. Worded less grandly, they were both daily drudges. The Italian Renaissance theatre was a holiday theatre that flared with brief brilliance. It was more spectacular than steady.

NOTES

The headnote is taken from Heywood's *An Apology for Actors* (1612).

Clark's compendium of criticism provides the Scaliger quotation (p. 61) and Castelvetro's arguments (p. 64); Cinthio's estimate of Seneca is found in Herrick's *Italian Tragedy* (p. 73); Aretino's remarks are given by Prezzolini (p. 127); Ben Jonson on poetry and picture is quoted in *Ben Jonson; Selected Works,* edited by Harry Levin (published by Random House, New York, 1938), p. 977; Lope de Vega is quoted by Clark, p. 89.

Clark, Herrick, Kennard, and Prezzolini were the chief suppliers of the material in this chapter. Details of these books are provided in the bibliography.

Chapter IV

SERLIO'S STAGE

. . . a stage set forth with pomp and pride
Where rich men cost and cunning art bestow
When curtains be removed that all did hide,
Doth make by light of torch a glittering show.
—LODOVICO ARIOSTO

In a period when the authors of plays and dramatic criticism were haunted by writers and critics who had been dead for 1,500 years, we should not be surprised to find the shades of classic ideas about production lurking backstage as well. Classic lore about theatre and stage was less abundant but quite as powerful. The chief ghost to haunt this realm was the Roman architect Marcus Vitruvius Pollio, who wrote his *De architectura* late in the first century before Christ. Although his treatment of theatre was a minor part of his work, it exerted an influence that would be hard to imagine or credit if we did not know of the similarly prepossessing influence of Seneca in Renaissance Italy. He was some ghost. First published at Rome in 1486, Vitruvius begat a series of editions, translations, and major commentaries that numbered at least thirty in the sixteenth century. His influence in theatre construction and stage arrangement was palpable before his work appeared in print. A manuscript copy had been rediscovered in 1414, and from that time on Vitruvius was the Renaissance architect's chief study. Such an architect was Leon Battista Alberti, who applied his knowledge of Vitruvius and his own study of classic ruins to the construction of a short-lived theatre for Pope Nicholas V in

1452. The courtyard theatre and stage set up by Prisciani in 1486 for the production of *Menaechmi* at Ferrara reflected similar studies.

Vitruvius' treatise dealt briefly with the theatre, and without an extant unruined theatre to refer to, it probably was not as clear as might be wished. His discussion of the use of scenery was briefer. This is a happy circumstance, for in his brevity and lack of clarity about stage arrangement lay a measure of freedom for the Renaissance architect, a measure of freedom denied the playwrights, especially the writers of tragedy, who extracted from their classic texts more definite formulas. Vitruvius implied more than he specified. For instance, his discussion of machines ("efficacious in moving great weights") gave authority, if any were needed, for the later architects to play with them and devise them. His statement that "every year both *praetors* and *aediles* have to provide machinery for the festivals" helped make theatre activity the business of princes. Admired Rome had given that responsibility to its great ones, and so a Renaissance prince could not be confident he was so worthy unless he did the same. Theatre was the business of princes. Machiavelli recommended that a prince who wished to be considered excellent "should engage the attention of the people with festivals and shows." Savonarola wrote of the same deed as they policy of a tyrant. Both writers reflect the same idea of theatre as an affair of political value. Vitruvius' very inclusion of theatre and scenery in his treatise confirmed the assignment of the court architect to one more job along with building palaces, churches, harbors, canals, fortifications, and so on; architects became stage designers.

The Roman theatre these architects looked upon as ideal had three parts: a long, low acting platform or stage, a scenic facade backing the stage, and an auditorium laid out in semicircular form. A flat half-circle at the lowest level of the auditorium was the Roman remainder of the Greek orchestra, a fully circular dancing place where the chorus had performed. Surrounding this semicircular Roman orchestra was the amphitheatre seating, rising in tiers to a great height in order to accommodate a huge crowd. The scenic facade backing the stage rose to the full height of this large open-air structure in a showy elaboration of columns, pediments, pilasters, niches, and statues—an impressive display of festive immensity. This magnificent, declarative architecture provided five entrances onto the stage. There were three main entrance doors facing the auditorium and two doors at the extreme ends of the stage set at right angles to the stage front, that is, what we call the curtain line.

In laying out a theatre, Vitruvius advised the architect to inscribe four equilateral triangles within a circle and so mark twelve equidistant points on the circumference. This circle was to be as great in diameter as the straight edge of the semicircular orchestra. Two of the twelve circumference points were used to bisect the circle and establish both the line of the stage platform and the line of the straight edge of the semicircular orchestra. The five points on one

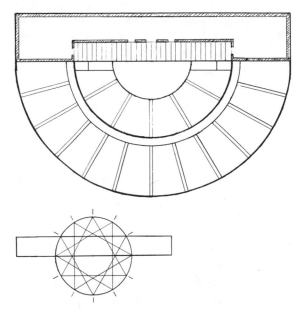

Fig. 10. *Plan of a Roman theatre.*

side of the circle would indicate the location of the radiating aisles in the amphitheatre. Five points on the circle remained. Those three farthest away from the diameter line of the orchestra helped locate the central or royal door and the two flanking secondary doors in the scenic facade. The two remaining points nearest the diameter line established the line of the scenic facade and in locating it determined how deep the stage was to be. The facade was extended so that its width would be double that of the diameter of the original circle. This left room for a stage platform between the line of the facade and the line of the orchestra's straight edge that was comparatively long but narrow, wide but not deep, with scenery (the facade) behind the stage and the semicircular orchestra in front.

Constructed in the courtyard of a ducal palace, a theatre of this sort probably was not as curious as it became when moved indoors. When theatres were set up inside the court, inside the large halls of princes, as they probably soon were, for most plays were performed at the wintry carnival time before Lent (we have already cited the canceled pageant of Hercules' labors at a rained-on performance of *Amphitruo* in Duke Ercole's courtyard in 1487), the Renaissance versions of these theatres became round pegs in square holes. But architects and their patrons seem to have been happier with their fidelity to their classic blueprint than dismayed at the capricious union of the semicircle and the rectangle. An edition of Vitruvius published at Venice in 1513 illustrated the arrangement with plans that clearly enclosed the semicircular auditorium within a rectangle. Sebastiano Serlio, in his architectural book of 1545, saw the problem and contentedly noted that "although halls (however large they may be) could not accommodate theatres such as the ancients had, nevertheless in order to follow the ancients as closely as possible, I have included in my plan such parts of the ancient theatre as a great hall might contain." Serlio's plan shows the semicircular auditorium cut off by the walls of the hall; only those rows or tiers in the amphitheatre that are close to the orchestra are fully semicircular. A large outdoor theatre, conceived on a huge scale, was jammed inside a hall because it was thought important to "follow the ancients as closely as possible." A larger hall rather than a more modest model was wished for. "The greater the hall," Serlio wrote, "the more nearly will the theatre assume its perfect form."

Like the first-made auditoriums, the stage platforms conformed to the Vitruvian model. Their narrow depth and long width are the more curious because the Renaissance architect was doing something new with the stage: he was using it in a way that had some classic warrant but no specific instructions. He was backing that stage not with an ornate, formal architectural facade but with a perspective setting which, it would seem, needed more working depth than a stage based on the points of the Vitruvian circle allowed.

Architecture included scenic design as well as theatre design, and the former included perspective. For Vitruvius passed on the tradition that Agatharcus had painted a perspective scene for Aeschylus, and he passed on the news that Democritus and Anaxagoras had written of perspective "showing how, given a center in a definite place, the lines should naturally correspond with due regard to the point of sight and the divergence of the visual rays, so that by this deception a faithful representation of the appearance of buildings might be given in painted scenery, and . . . though all is drawn on a vertical flat facade, some parts may seem to be withdrawing . . . and others to be standing out." So much was enough to turn the Renaissance version of the Roman facade into scenery, into a kind of ideal painting-architecture that, through the use of perspective, realized visions of "cloud-capp'd towers . . . gorgeous palaces . . . solemn temples." The great artists of the period had toiled and toyed with perspective for some time; now it was applied to the stage.

The Ferrarese productions of 1508 were the first of which we have a clear account of this application. Pellegrino's "view in perspective of a town with houses, churches, belfries and gardens" was "most cleverly designed and executed." When *Calandria* was first given at Urbino in 1513, one of the most notable of scenic artists, Girolamo Genga, set the stage in a way that elicited a glowing appreciation. It was "a very beautiful city with streets, palaces, churches and towers . . . there was an octagonal temple in low relief so well finished that it seems hardly possible that it could have been built in four months even if one considers all the potential workmanship which the state of Urbino can muster." Windows seemed made of alabaster, architraves and

cornices of "fine gold and ultramarine blue." Pieces of glass imitated jewels and "looked like genuine gems." Pillars and statues "simulated marble." Similarly, Baldassare Peruzzi set the scene for *Calandria* the next year at Rome for Pope Leo. Vasari recorded it was "wonderful how, in the narrow space, he depicted his streets, palaces, and curious temples, loggias and cornices." Wonders "in the narrow space," for at this time the stage was confined to the narrow ledge of the Roman model, confined within a segment of a semicircle.

Peruzzi died in 1537, leaving notes and drawings for a projected edition of Vitruvius to his pupil, Sebastiano Serlio. And so Serlio's *Regole generali di architettura* was published a book or two at a time at Venice, Paris, and Lyons over a period extending from 1537 to 1551. It may be taken as a guide to what sixteenth-century scenic artists were doing, particularly his Book Two, published in 1545, which treated of perspective and contained a brief discussion of stage matters and, more interestingly, a cross section and plan of a theatre and three scenic designs. Serlio did not put forth novel or unique ideas; he summarized and defined the usual practice of his time. The kind of stage set up by Genga at Urbino, Peruzzi and Raphael at Rome, and Pellegrino and Dossi at Ferrara is preserved in the Serlian storehouse. Serlio (1475–1554) was a contemporary of Ariosto (1474–1533).

The stage described by Serlio had two major parts. An acting platform took up half the visible depth of the stage. Serlio had built a theatre at Vicenza in 1530, and he records that the acting platform was about 60 feet wide but only about 12 feet deep. His book plan showed an acting platform over 80 feet wide if 12 feet is its depth. The acting platform was raised to eye level. We must isolate this long, narrow, high acting platform in our mind's

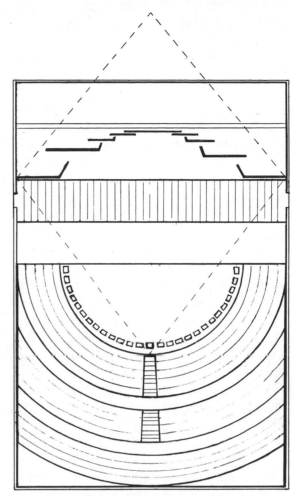

FIG. 11. *Plan of Serlio's stage and auditorium.*

eye, for on Serlio's bipartite stage, acting does not take place within a setting but on a distinctly separate acting platform in front of the scenery. Actors have often used no more. It seems apt to cite a passage from Giraudoux's *Impromptu de Paris* here. In it two actors discuss their notion that staging should be kept simple. "All that's needed is a space where we can be heard—a solid floor under our feet," says one. The other asks for "a base—like a gun emplacement. Then fire away!" Serlio's acting platform meets these demands. However, his stage was the work of architects, not actors, and so immediately behind the acting platform was a scenic platform.

This second part of the stage was a raked platform about the same depth as the first, no more than 13 feet, on which was arranged the perspective scenery. This scenery was arranged and painted to give an illusion of much greater depth. On each side, the buildings or houses presented in the scene, varied by their architectural features and proportions, were painted on angle wings. That is, each unit making up the scene, each house, had two sides: a front face (facing the auditorium) and a smaller perspective face which joined the onstage edge of the front face at an angle greater than 90 degrees. Each unit of the scene was, therefore, a two-sided angle wing. The angle was determined by the placement of the vanishing point of the perspective scheme, a nicely calculated central point some distance behind the scene. The top of the angled perspective face tapered down on a line conforming with the perspective scheme, and the bottom tapered up. Serlio recommended that the raked stage slope up one unit in nine of its depth. If the raked platform were 9 feet deep, it would rise so that it was 1 foot higher at its back edge. (Although our stages today are usually flat, from this raked stage we derive our modern terminology: "upstage," referring to that part of the stage farthest from the audience, and "downstage," referring to that part closest to the audience.) The front face of an angle wing was a rectangle. The perspective face was a trapezoid with its top and bottom edges conforming to the perspective lines that moved toward the vanishing point of the perspective. Diminished in size, the perspective face's painted details (its windows, doors, balconies, cornices) also diminished in exact proportion to their distance from the front face. A short distance behind the first pair of down-

stage angle wings on either side of the scenic platform, another pair was placed. Serlio recommended that the second wing be built and painted to resemble a larger house or building that might tower above the first. In this way, more of this second building would be visible. But if it were "bigger," its architectural features would, of course, be painted proportionately "smaller" in order to create the illusion that it was much farther away. Other pairs of angle wings were placed behind the second, and so on, to the end of the shallow depth of that part of the stage devoted to the scenery. The perspective face of each would be positioned on a line that went upstage on an angle, not directly but on a slant toward the central vanishing point. Serlio's plan showed four angle wings on each side. Upstage, a flat unit with other buildings painted on its single flat surface finished the scene. This final scenic unit could be flat because its ends were out of sight, masked by the side angle wings in front of its extreme edges. There also was a theoretical reason for its flatness: objects far away appear less round or solid than objects near at hand. "If the house is set very far to the back," Serlio wrote, "one frame will be sufficient so long as all its

FIG. 12. *Design for the "Tragic Scene," Serlio, 1545. Theatre Arts Prints.*

parts are skillfully designed and painted." So it is in nature: distant objects—mountains, buildings, even cylindrical shapes—appear flat.

An audience seated before such a scene had the illusion of being in the middle of a city street, looking down it past the buildings on either side and seeing farther to a great distance. Serlio's sample scene drawings and a Peruzzi street scene preserved at Florence give us this sense of distance and do not hint at the narrow confines of the scenic platform on which they were placed. Serlio commented that he could have shown grander edifices if he had had more space. It is odd that he knew this well enough to state it, yet worked on a shallow scenic stage that narrowly conformed to the Vitruvian model. Contemporary testimony, however, sings the refrain of grandeur successfully conveyed.

Time and money were lavished on these scenes. In describing them and the princely patrons who paid the cost of these outward and visible signs of their status, the recurring word is "magnificence." Vasari's description of Peruzzi's work affirmed that, properly staged, comedies "surpass all other spectacular displays in magnificence." When Serlio advised that "the more costly these things are, the more they are worthy of praise," he does not sound like a scenic artist with a mingy budget. An expensive show expressed "the generosity of rich lords and their enmity to ugly stinginess." Leone di Somi, a Mantuan director and the author of four dialogues dealing with the stage written some twenty years after Serlio, mentioned a magnificent court setting which was destroyed after its brief hour of use. "The greater was (the duke's) magnanimity in spending so many thousands on that marvelous set and then destroying it when it had served its immediate purpose." The purpose was the celebration of the duke's marriage.

The devisers of these settings developed techniques for lighting and prettifying them. Special glass containers held colored water in front of lamps so that the light was tinged with blue, emerald, and ruby. Barber's basins were polished and set up to reflect the beams more brightly. Di Somi wrote of using mirrors to multiply the light because they did not smoke and blur the scene as extra lamps would have done. Innumerable lamps were wanted to provide the brightest light possible. Di Somi also devised ways to dim the lights to help convey the mood of somber moments in the play, an important trick when a tragedy was performed. Metal cylinders were lowered over the candle or lamp flame to obstruct the beams. Colored glass was placed in the panes of house windows. Statues, cut from cardboard or thin wood and placed far back in the scene where no one had a side view of them, were painted to look like marble or bronze.

The earliest pictorial evidence of a proscenium arch framing a stage setting seems to be a design by Bartolomeo Neroni for a production of *L'Ortensio* at Siena in 1560. Neroni built a theatre for the Intronati Academy there in that year. His setting placed behind an elaborate proscenium arch is of a city street, painted on angle wings in the manner described by Serlio. But surely the proscenium arch appeared much earlier than this particular pictorial evidence. It appears much earlier in pictures of street tableaux, and a description of the *Calandria* production of 1513 rather certainly includes a proscenium arch. Serlio does not mention or picture it, but it is implied in his arrangement. The first angle wing defined the picture plane, and a drapery valance or cornice would have masked the edges of the scenic units, which were painted to resemble the sky and hung above the setting. No illusion of depth would have been possible unless the walls and ceiling of the hall (where the stage was erected) beyond the first pair of angle wings were hidden. Some masking piece above would also have hidden the lights atop the setting and shielded the spectators from their glare.

A curtain was used in these shows to hide the scene while the audience assembled. Then, usually with trumpeting music, it dropped in the impressive manner of a sudden revelation to expose the brightly lit marvel behind. Some curtains were painted perspectively and were admired in the interval before the entertainment began. Pope Leo adjusted his glasses to "enjoy" a curtain so painted by Raphael. Contrary to modern theatre practice, front curtains were not used during the course of the play to mark act or scene divisions or for any other purpose.

Also contrary to our practice, as has been mentioned, the actors did not play in the scene but were mostly confined to the acting platform in front. They were advised by di Somi to "avoid getting too close to the scenic perspectives" lest by getting too near, the scene would lose "verisimilitude." Any gadding about upstage would have either diminished the houses or magnified the actors. One canny director wrote that ghosts might best be placed upstage where their seemingly tremendous size would make them more terrifying. From di Somi's writing we get the impression that a decent delivery, a graceful carriage, and modest gestures were enough for an actor, although some show of spirit would not have been amiss. Di Somi wrote, "It is always well for them to act as much in the middle of the stage and on the proscenium line (meaning the front edge of the platform) as possible, and to face the spectators." This is advice only demure amateurs would need; downstage center is, of course, exactly where actors want to be.

Costuming was elaborate, colorful, and rich. It must have added a good deal to the show. "I would not hesitate to dress a servant in velvet or colored satin provided . . . (his) master's costume had sufficient embroidery and gold ornament to make a proper distinction between them." Thus, di Somi expressed how to costume in a way that may be summarized: the rich get richer and the poor rich.

The auditorium depicted by Serlio was more Roman than his stage. In front and below the acting platform was a rectangular area of about the same size called the proscenium, or, more poetically, *la piazza della scena*. It was the only area in the hall that was not elevated or built up when a stage and theatre were erected, and it seemed to serve no purpose other than to place the audience at a greater distance from the perspective, which would look less "forced" if viewed from a distance. Then there was a semicircular orchestra 6 inches above floor level which was ringed by seats reserved for the nobility, who in Serlio's plan numbered twenty-seven. The central seat would afford the best view of the perspective. Indeed, it is hard to imagine how the scene had perfect coherence if viewed off-center or if the beholder's eye point was much above or below the level of the scene's vanishing point. The perspective lines would be askew from anywhere else. In a double sense, Serlio's arrangement was fit for a king. The coming age of monarchical absolutism had a place prepared for it in a theatre in which the royal throne was the auditorium's central feature. Mathematical calculations for the whole arrangement had their zero point there. Castelvetro's critical *dicta* about the "scene of action" being confined to "that one place alone which could be visible to one person" may be forgiven him when perspective scenes are the thing. Now we know where the one place is and who the one person is.

Farther away, behind Serlio's twenty-seven, were banked tiers of seats in an amphitheatre having three sections, the first completely semicircular and the arcs of the second and third cut off by the rectangular confines of the hall. The first section was for the ladies, "most noble ladies" in front and those of lesser rank "higher up." A hundred years later, the architect Nicola Sabbattini suggested that the central seats of the first section be reserved for the most beautiful ladies. I suppose he meant them to be noble as well. Noble or ignoble, beauties so bestowed had an effect, according to Sabbattini. "Those who are acting and striving to please . . . (would gain) inspiration from this lovely prospect, perform more gaily, with greater assurance, and with greater zest." A discreet official who supervised the seating arrangements was to separate the sheep from the goats. If di Somi had so arranged things, his advice to the actors to "face the spectators" was redundant. Serlio's second section was for noblemen, his third section for men of lesser rank, and there was space for the common people high up at the back in a space between the last arc of seats and the wall of the hall.

When we consider how much the Italians of this time loved pictures and spectacle, the early sixteenth-century stage seems oddly static. There it was, impressively decorated, fascinating in its presentation of a perspective vista crowded with the architecture of an ideal city, lit by colored lights, decked with reasonable facsimiles of marble, bronze, and jewels, but static with no scene changes. If it seemed to them becomingly correct in its approach to the Roman model, it had not as much room as a convincing perspective stage would seem to require. For that, a deeper stage was wanted. The classic warrant for perspective had been written by the same hand that withheld an easy depth in which to work. But the Italian scenic artists were not held so long in bondage to the classic mold as were the playwrights. How they broke this static mold, created a new and deeper stage, and placed changeable scenery upon that stage is another part of our story.

Here it is enough to remind ourselves that from the very beginning the Italians livened and lengthened their plays and perhaps relieved what may have been the monotony of repetitive Plautine revivals with dance and musical intermezzi that featured performers costumed in rich and bizarre raiment. One of Isabella d'Este's belittling notes of the 1502 festival described a night impoverished of intermezzi. "Last night only two dances were introduced in the play, and at the end we heard nothing but groans and complaints from the spectators." Soon it was the general practice that between the regulation five acts, mythological, allegorical, pastoral, historical, horrible, and wondrously beautiful creatures danced, sang, and displayed themselves on the platform before the street scene. Although the burden of their songs and dances were often unrelated to the play, they were appropriate in their exotic way, true in their fashion, to the occasion the court celebrated. Fantastic, varied, and colorful, they added a dimension the spectacle would not otherwise have had in this age that revered the classic unities. It is pleasant to notice that this age was willing to turn away from that dull reverence, backsliding for the bright interval of an intermezzo.

Serlio described a stage scene that impressed him greatly. In its context, his paragraph comes at the end of a passage echoing Vitruvius. The assumption of both architects is that plays should be given an appropriate background, not necessarily a setting for a particular play but a setting for the *kind* of play it happened to be. Thus, Vitruvius: "There are three kinds of scenes,

FIG. 13. *Design for the "Satyric Scene," by Serlio, 1545. Theatre Arts Prints.*

one called tragic, second, the comic, third, the satyric. Their decorations are different and unlike each other in scheme. Tragic scenes are delineated with columns, pediments, statues, and other objects suited to kings; comic scenes exhibit private dwellings, with balconies and views representing rows of windows, after the manner of ordinary dwellings." Fifteen hundred years later Serlio reversed this order and wrote of the comic scene first. Could this have been because he and his fellow architects were most often asked to provide a stage for comedy? "The comic scene has houses appropriate to private persons, as citizens, lawyers, merchants, parasites and other similar persons. Above all, the scene should have its house of the procuress, its tavern, and its church." As for the tragic scene, "Its houses must be those of great persons . . . stately houses."

Vitruvius wrote of decorating the satyric scene "with trees, caverns, mountains, and other rustic objects delineated in landscape style." With no exact counterpart of satyric plays, unless it was the disputes of shep-

herds in eclogues or other approaches to the pastoral play, Serlio summoned Roman authority and wrote that Vitruvius "recommends that these scenes be composed of trees, rocks, hills, mountains, herbs, flowers, and fountains." After noting that leafy trees and flowers are not available during carnival season, when plays were given, Serlio recommends they be made of silk and then, moving away from Vitruvius, he describes such a scene which he had seen at Urbino. We sense that here is a Renaissance artist less in awe of Rome, a man proud of what his generation could do. Serlio's drawing of the satyric scene shows a perspective composed without the regularity of his street scenes for comedy or tragedy, without the uniform placement of paired angle wings. It is a mansion of natural detail which he celebrates:

Some time ago my eyes beheld such scenes carried out by the architect Girolamo Genga at the instance of his lord, Francesco Maria, Duke of Urbino. (Serlio and Genga were both at Urbino around 1525.) In these I witnessed as much liberality in the prince as taste and skill in the architect. Such beauty was there in the setting as I have never seen in any other similar work. Oh immortal God! what wonder it was to see so many trees and fruits, so many herbs and diverse flowers, all made from the finest silk of the most beautiful colors, the cliffs and rocks covered with diverse sea shells, with snails and other animals, with coral branches of many colors, with sea crabs among the rocks, with so great diversity of beautious things that to write about all of them would take too long. I will not speak of the costumes of satyrs, nymphs, and sirens or of the shapes of monsters and strange animals, skillfully constructed to be worn by men and children according to their size. The movements of the actors seemed to bring these animals to life, each according to its own nature. And if it were not that I should prove too prolix, I should tell of the superb

FIG. 14. *Molière's* The School for Husbands, *adapted by Lawrence Langer and Arthur Guiterman, and designed for the Theatre Guild production by Lee Simonson in 1934, had a setting reminiscent of Serlio. Theatre Arts Prints.*

costumes of some shepherds made of rich cloth of gold and silk, furred with the finest skins of wild animals. I could speak also of the costumes of some fishermen which were no less rich than the others, whose nets were of thread of fine gold and whose other tackle was all gilded. I could also describe some shepherdesses whose costumes put avarice to shame. But all these things I leave to the taste and judgement of the architects, who will always be able to make things of this sort when they find similar patrons, generously willing to give them full license to carry out all they desire.

NOTES

The headnote is from Ariosto's thirty-second canto of *Orlando Furioso,* as translated by Sir John Harington.

Vitruvius is quoted from *Vitruvius, The Ten Books on Architecture,* translated by Morris Hickey Morgan, Cambridge: Harvard University Press, 1926, and used with their permission. See specifically pp. 282–283 on machines, p. 198 on perspective, and p. 150 on the three kinds of scene. Serlian doctrine appears in the translation of Allardyce Nicoll in *The Renaissance Stage,* edited by Barnard Hewitt, published by the University of Miami Press. All of the quotations occur on pp. 27–29 except for the description of Genga's scene at Urbino, which is on p. 32 of this valuable book. The publishers have given me permission to quote from it.

Gilbert cites Machiavelli on princely theatre, p. 167; Nagler's *Sourcebook* gives descriptions of the *Calandria* productions, pp. 71–72; Giraudoux's *Impromptu,* translated by Rima Drell Rick, appears in *Tulane Drama Review,* Vol. 3, No. 4, May 1959, pp. 107–128; Vasari on Peruzzi is quoted on p. 51 of Campbell; Nicoll's *Development* provides transla-

tions of di Somi on expensive theatrics (p. 258), on actor's positions (p. 256), and on costuming (p. 262); Sabbattini is quoted from Hewitt, p. 96, and Isabella's complaint is taken from Cartwright, p. 208.

I should cite, in addition to the works named above, Beijer's article in *Theatre Research.* It was of particular use in writing this chapter. See also Kernodle's *From Art to Theatre.*

Chapter V

COMMEDIA DELL'ARTE

The cheefe actors had not their parts fully penned, but spoke much extemporary or upon agreement betweene themselves, espetially the wemen, whose speeches were full of wantoness, though not grosse baudy . . . . Their plays were of amorous matters.

—FYNES MORYSON

While the courts were generously willing to lavish their treasure on their re-created Roman plays, their re-created Roman stage, and their bright new intermezzi, while they used the stage as a testament of their "enmity to ugly stinginess," there was scarcely an Italian theatre outside of the courts. Putting "avarice to shame," the court theatres spluttered to a gorgeous glow within a rhythm set by peacetime carnival seasons and the advent of princely marriages, embassies, and visitations. While court poets received some patronage and notice, and while some pride was felt in the retention of an inventive architect, few actors or performers are recorded or mentioned and few or none of the professional companies. O strange new theatre that had such goodly architects in it!

Italian actors could not have been idle. If at first not professional, they were amateurs; if they did not perform at court, then they did so on a set of planks in the public square. If not paid to pronounce the flatteries addressed to princes, they extolled the sovereign salve of a mountebank. They were preparing a vulgar, lively theatre founded on an art as old as the impulse to entertain. If there was little promise in

plays that had the esteemed Senecan smell, the proper academic aura, they took their own counsel and their dialogue of "you say this and I'll say that and then we'll do this" created the matter for a scene, and then a play developed whose every part had been tested in the arena of audience response. Words can only rudely paraphrase the central learning of theatre art; no book illuminates as much as is written in the exchange of performer and audience.

The unknown actors of the early sixteenth century were not without art, for they were also humanist children of the Renaissance and the plots they devised for their comedy were based in classic work, as were their figures of speech, their tricks of mind, and their disposition to the stage. But they digested Rome for what juice was in it. Rome was subordinated to a freer impulse than the players could have felt from the patronage of a prince with a roomful of professors by his side. When their art had matured, they were cherished. But no one city or court sustained them for long. So traveling from one to another, they crossed borders of countries and became international. Their form of theatre was improvised comedy, and they became famous as the Italian comedians, the creators of commedia dell'arte.

This new and unique theatre form suddenly and distinctly appeared; it had developed unheralded and unsung and no man recorded whence or whither or the hour of its coming. Only those conditioned by ballyhoo expect the wave of the future to be conspicuous and beat its own drum. Confronted by its unknown origin, scholars have been tempted to find a missing link that could at least be expressed by a cautious double negative. (Great is the reward in academe when possible sources can be proposed.) So some have discovered it is "not unlikely" that commedia dell'arte is really the Roman mime renascent. In some untraceable way, it represents survival. We know the Dark Ages were not so glum as to forbid the brief candle of a player. In Byzantium, if nowhere else, the mime persisted, and mimes joined the Greek scholars who fled to a more congenial Christian Europe at the fall of Constantinople in 1453. The learned ones and their books affected humanistic learning. The survival and exodus of the mimes and their skills explain the reappearance of professional players in Italy. The source hounds add their notes of comparison: the form, the type of entertainment, the characters or masks of commedia put them in mind of the mime and of the more ancient Atellan farce.

Atellan farce was a popular theatre form developed in the Campania south of Rome in the years before the Christian era. It has been celebrated as a distinctly Italian form of comedy, unlike most Roman dramatic forms, which were adapted from Greek rather than derived from native sources. At first apparently improvised, fragments of a later literary form of Atellan farce have survived and so have over one hundred titles of the short plays. In some ways it is strikingly like commedia dell'arte. It had a

gallery of stock characters who appeared in different plays: grandad Pappus, clowns Maccus and Bucco, hunchback Dossennus, Manducus, who may have been an ogre with clamping jaws, and Cicirrus, perhaps a soldier (fighting cock). All these were masked misbehavers. Maccus became the chief figure of the literary form as titles like "Maccus, the Soldier," "Maccus, the Innkeeper," and "Maccus, the Maid" suggest. Although Atellan farce is not mentioned after the first century, its stock characters, improvisation, and masks make it seem a likely forebear of commedia dell'arte, even if it was only kept alive by the mimes, who embraced in their nebulous form all sorts of theatrical and amusing turns.

That the commedia, alone of all modern European theatre forms, used masks is a convincing argument that it represents survival. Yet the masks are different from those of antiquity, which seem to have all been full-faced. Commedia used smaller caricaturing masks. One other difference is that Atellan farce seems to have been done solely by men, whereas the commedia had women in its troupes. So did the mimes, however.

So we come back to our puzzle and hedge by writing that commedia dell'arte may have represented survival. But need we be reluctant to grant anyone an idea of his own? Need we be uneasy if we can clutch no reassuring source? Could the commedia have been an invention of sixteenth-century Italians, a humble, simple thing, born of amateur effort, nurtured by semi-professionals, and given final form by professionals, all in a rather short time?

There is some truth of what might have been, something of an insight, in a note made of a lecture by Coleridge. "Mr. C., in Italy, heard a quack in the street, who was accosted by his servant smartly; a dialogue ensued which pleased the mob; the next day the quack, having perceived the good effect of an adjunct, hired a boy to talk with him. In this way a play might have originated."

There probably was more survival than has been recorded. In 1364 Petrarch wrote of festivities at Venice celebrating the conquest of Crete and that one Tommaso Bambasio, "who throughout the state of Venice has the reputation that Roscius formerly had in Rome and is to me as dear a friend as Roscius was to Cicero," was sent for from Ferrara to participate in the merriment. We infer that Bambasio was a professional player. Petrarch intrigues us with this solitary mention and with Bambasio's having come from Ferrara, but no record of career or companions survives. That there was farce among the peasants and so gutsy a title as this from Asti, *Farce of Zolan Zavatino and of Beatrix His Wife and of the Priest Hidden Under the Poultry Basket,* is, to say the least, suggestive. Yet we cannot say of the Roscius of his age nor of peasant farces that they were descendants of mime, nor can we any more certainly label them precursors of commedia.

There are records of early sixteenth-century entertainers like Zan Polo, a Venetian who wrote comedy, danced, made music, tumbled, and entertained with mimicry. His son, Cimador, had a similar bag of tricks. Angelo Beolco, a Paduan whom we mentioned in our discussion of Ferrara, had his semiprofessional carnival season company in the 1520's. There are records of later companies of players, such as one formed at Siena in 1531. In 1543 Maphio dei Re, another Paduan, became the leader of a traveling company, and there are records of his fellow players' agreements to buy a mule for costume transport, to travel, and to govern themselves. The eight men who formed this company later included a boy to play women's roles. Their leader

was killed in a brawl in Rome in 1553. None of these companies can certainly be labeled commedia dell'arte. However, their existence proves a development of professional playing, a groundbreaking for the commedia troupes to come.

At Mantua in 1568 there appears the first record of the first famous performer of commedia dell'arte, Alberto Naseli, renowned by his stage name of Zan Ganassa. His career was a blend of performer, entertainer, play-maker, and entrepreneur. He could appear with a tumbling Spaniard "during the sweet meat course" at a marriage banquet at Ferrara and the next year perform plays at Lyons and the next at Paris. There in 1572 he appeared with a repertoire of plays performed by six companions who could provide acrobatic turns as well as improvise a comedy. Ganassa may have taken his company to London in 1574. That year some enterprising Italians crossed the channel and gave an English preacher the opportunity to deplore that London should witness such a spectacle as the "unchaste, shamelesse and unnatural tomblinge of the Italian women." If these nimble nymphs were Ganassa's, he soon took them off to Spain, for later that year of 1574 he set his seal on a transaction to fix up a stage in the *Corral de la Pacheca* in Madrid and committed his company to sixty performances. This Italian venturer and six or seven companions were variously at Madrid and Seville for almost a decade thereafter. Zan Ganassa was clearly a performer in the commedia dell'arte mode and for want of anything more certain to do about a date, we might call the year of his first mention, 1568, the year of commedia's beginning.

However, there are records of other activity the year of 1568 in Bologna and, of all places, Munich that indicate this kind of comedy had been rather well established beforehand. In Bologna the ecclesiastics sought in written protest to forestall "a thousand sins" provoked by "Zani's comedies" and to protect the "young men and boys" of the city from performances where courtesans mingled. The shows were criticized as "lascivious, dishonest pieces which corrupt good morals" and (if the clerics are to be believed) were performed by "vagabonds of evil repute, who carry about with them women of bad life." To remedy this situation, the comedians were to be restricted to thrice-weekly performances and forbidden to advertise in the streets with their drums and alluring costumes.

In Bavaria, more happily for all, a Neapolitan musician at the court threw together at the suggestion of Duke William a wedding entertainment which he called a *"commedia improvisa all'Italiana."* He was

FIG. 15. *Painting by Paul Porbus, 1572, of a commedia dell'arte troupe at the court of King Charles IX. (Bayeux Museum.) In this lively group, the king and the duke of Guise are engaged in a mock quarrel over a kneeling amorosa. Pantalone stands near them looking hangdog. Above him is Catherine de Medici and behind him is Arlecchino in the first known painting of that immortal mask. The future King Henry III is the man farthest upstage. If, as some scholars believe, it is the troupe of Alberto Naseli that is here surrounded by the Valois Court, the zany on the left with his hand on the breast of the maid is Zan Ganassa and the Pantalone is Stefanello Bottarga, a great actor of the Venetian. Theatre Arts Prints.*

Massimo Troiano and he rehearsed seven improvising amateurs in a ten-character play. The duke's organist, a Fleming, collaborated with Troiano and played the Venetian *magnifico* (Pantalone). The Zanni (the clown) was played by a goldsmith, Baptista Scholari. These sportive musicians prepared themselves in less than two days. We take Troiano's word that they did well. We can be sure that by 1568 commedia was established and that at least several of Troiano's companions and the duke himself had an easy familiarity with it. Clearly, the commedia had come to be some time before 1568.

We think of commedia as the base-born child of the Renaissance, spawned in the streets and public squares, a wild urchin dressed in the ragged raiment of tricks and jokes and wanton wiles that rogues and vagabonds fashion to filch the popular penny. That is what it appears to have been at Bologna. The English traveler Thomas Coryat in Venice in 1608 recorded how five or six mountebanks in noisy competition erected stages in the Piazza San Marco and with music and clowns brought a crowd to focus on the medicinal contents of an enormous trunk that seems to have been the notable property of their stage. At length the mountebank in familiar and fascinating bamboozle did "most hyperbolically extoll the virtue of his drugs and confections."

There is, or was when I was green, a counterpart of this commedia in the traveling medicine show which erected its rude platform in the cow pasture of a rural Pennsylvania town. As I recall, a series of comedy sketches was acted by a small company whose sallies and wit we rubes enjoyed. Sample: the "boss" in a Prince Albert coat and striped trousers demanded that the black porter hold his tongue, and the clown did. It seems odd to me that I was once so simple as to enjoy that gag so much. There was a fascinating lady unlike any I had ever seen who wore bright yellow tights and could do awesome contortions and acrobatics for an entr'acte. Before, during, and after the comedy, candy and surprise packages were hawked among the standing crowd and around a parked semicircle of Fords and Chevvies. The chief item for sale was a nostrum made from a genuine Indian recipe that the man in the Prince Albert outfit plausibly claimed would alleviate a long list of symptoms, complaints, and melancholic tendencies. I could not understand my father's refusal to snap up the bargain. Such scenes are surely half as old as time.

In 1598 two students at Avignon found commedia dell'arte troupes holding forth. The students recorded that the best of them had four actors and two actresses performing on a stage in a rented tennis court. Those outside in the public square drew "a thousand spectators" with a comedy lasting an hour or two followed by a Pantalone and Doctor who brought to public attention the marvelous contents of their trunk. Money was passed up and medicine passed down, and sometimes there came from the stage an actress' note agreeing to meet some fellow who seemed both taken with her and worth her taking. Many performers developed and many elements of commedia grew to their full realization in the rough-and-tumble of streets and fairs. These performers were used by purveyors of quack remedies who needed them to attract the gullible, and they in turn used the opportunity to learn the way of a performer with his audience.

Because commedia could be so vulgar and was so distinctly popular, we tend to think of it as unrelated to the court theatre. Its early mention at the Bavarian court should remind us of its other milieu. The relationship of commedia to court was more than a matter of sometime patronage. Con-

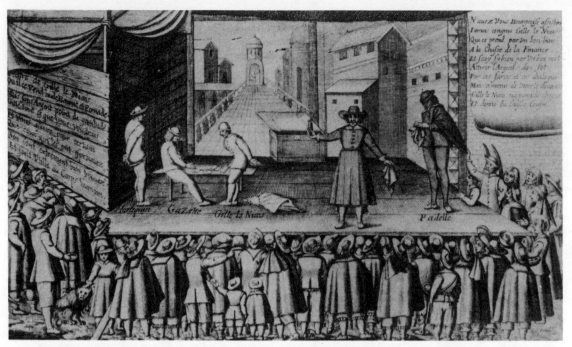

FIG. 16. *This print, made in Paris in 1640, shows the mountebank holding the attention of all but a boy and his dog. There is a perspective drop upstage of the medicine chest and advertisements appear at the sides. The clown figures onstage with the medico include Harlequin at left. From* The Stage Is Set *by Lee Simonson, published by Theatre Arts Books.*

sider a bit of absurdity recorded as taking place at Ferrara in 1582. Two of the most popular masks, the patient servant clown, Pedrolino, and the old man fusser, Pantalone, were set to work to liven a ducal banquet. Pedrolino bestowed himself in the midst of the diners baked in a pie, hardly a dainty dish to set before a duke. Pantalone came looking for his lost servant among the nobility. We can bring the moment alive if we entertain the idea of Jack Benny looking for Rochester at a very posh dinner to which Benny has been invited to play the violin. Imagine the impertinent comedy of a search for a foolish fellow among the munching Este. Hidden Pedrolino's voice suggests fantastic notions to Pantalone. A charming lady has suggested to me that when Pantalone found the errant servant, the obligatory demand, "What are you doing in that pie?" would have set

up the standard comeback, "What pie?" With the clowns' reward and hope of a return engagement at carnival time depending on an inventive wit, they would have trained themselves to see a situation and quickly decide its comic possibilities. They would have learned to sustain their act by creating a scene with a thread of plot to keep it going. Out of repartee would come plays. "And," saith the eternal showman, "what do we do for an encore?" On the spot to contrive, the players would have gone off on wild tacks and wasted motion, but they also would have found a richer course of study for the comedian than Aristotle or Horace hinted at. They would have learned what Lope de Vega called "the art which they devised who aspired to the applause of the crowd."

The court theatre was a school for the professional players in another way. At the festivals, the players were part of a larger scheme. From the back of the hall, where Serlio's theatre provided standing room for common people, they would have seen the correct courtly comedy or tragedy and the dazzling intermezzi. And they would have learned, unbemused by second-hand strictures from new-fangled *Poetics,* what kind of fare took with an audience. When the fresh young prince piping the prologue charmed his near relations, the professional may have been underwhelmed but he listened and learned. At such a time he would have exercised a discrimination which the noble ladies and gentlemen in the amphitheatre below and on the stage could hardly have imagined. For them the theatre was only part of a bright holiday; the professional whose livelihood was at stake observed with a glance that penetrated below the gaudy surface to the heart. Actors make fine audiences because they are alert for good things and the why and how of them. When they see something that fails to come off, they are attentive for the same reason. Indeed it is easier, for those with an alert curiosity, to learn, to be objective and analytical, when brought before something imperfectly done. They refine it in their imagination, sensing that one day they may do something like it and do it better. If these actors were not themselves scholars, if their experience of court shows amounted to a second-hand education in humanism and classic lore, the important thing is that they did acquire what amounted to an education.

From their experience as banquet clowns and from the observation of court plays, the professionals prepared to make the most of other opportunities the court might give. They sometimes acted in court plays, appeared in the intermezzi, and sometimes presented plays of their own making. There would be no set way or time for this to happen; one or another or all of these uses

of professional skill would be called for on occasion. The better performers and companies became the objects of solicitous, albeit erratic, patronage, and their work took on a refinement they might not have sought to develop in the streets.

One of the commedia's constant features was its brash irreverence. Even in polite circles, part of its appeal was its saucy pertness. There are anecdotes reflecting an insouciance like that of Tristano Martinelli, the first great Arlecchino, who addressed the queen of France familiarly as "Dear Gossip" and gave to Henry IV the title of "Secret Secretary to the Secret Cabinet of Madame Marie de Medici." At least the art was delicate—to josh the great without jarring their tempers. Court fools often have been suffered gladly and the naughty players were as welcome in the palace as in the street.

As a theatre form, commedia dell'arte means comedy improvised by a company of stock characters or masks. But this definition needs to be improved by enlargement and qualification.

The chief element of commedia dell'arte was improvisation. First, let us take time to note that the Italian word *improviso* can be used to express the idea of something appearing suddenly or unexpectedly. This is a bit different from the apparently similar word in English, which can connote something jerry-rigged or something made to serve when nothing better is at hand. The English sense of improvisation as something on the spur of the moment is closer to the original sense of the word. To improvise a play meant that to the skeletal bones of the scenario or plot outline, which was determined in advance, the performers brought the flesh of their own speech and verbal skill. Theoretically, the words were new-minted in the heat of the onstage exchange with partners in the scene. The tension of performance was a spur to prick spontaneity. Imagination more than memory marked the playing and gave it a lively energetic quality. Theoretically, the same plot, nicely tuned to the particular audience and its peculiar mood and improvised anew, could on a different occasion yield a different entertainment, as distinctly different as its new dialogue made it. A new audience meant new creation rather than old repetition, for an improviser revises. To him a new town means new jokes and a new time, new topics. To him, a court audience in the evening is quite different from the marketplace rowdies he may have dealt with in the afternoon, and he does a different thing for them. From him come sudden and surprising things. Within the limitations of the plot and their own skill, the performers were free to shape and sharpen, to create anew for each occasion and for each entrance.

Practically, performances could hardly have been all that improvised. Whether the actor wrote his own speeches or worked them out in his head, he would be sure to remember those that had worked well and would not have been so lavish as to waste a good witty thing on one unique performance. If he had made it and an audience had enjoyed it, he would use it many times. It could be readily altered to a new situation. Gags and jokes are more precious than rubies. That is why many of them are quite old.

The clowns, or zanni, had their lazzi, that is, certain bits of comic business, horseplay, antics, jokes, snatches of repartee, and, indeed, Yorick's gibes, gambols, songs, and "flashes of merriment that were wont to set the table in a roar." They might be elaborated to the extent of a self-contained scene or be only brief bits of acrobatics, shrugs, or grimaces. The lazzi were specially suited to the zanni who used them and polished them for one play as well as for reuse in another. The other commedia characters had their set speeches, or *concetti,* to express a mood, cap a scene, provide a brilliant tirade, and, like the zanni's lazzi, they were reusable in different plays. The performers were "always reading, always gathering beauties from books," sharpening phrases, adapting old things for new scenes, honing homilies and disquisitions. There is a story of an orator who was asked how he had prepared a brilliant extemporaneous speech, and he replied that all his life he had made ready for that moment. When the improvising actor invented on the spur of the moment, he was far from depending on dumb luck, and he was some distance from unpremeditated art. He came to the moment prepared.

The Italians labeled their written comedy *commedia erudita* and thus distinguished it from *commedia dell'arte, commedia a soggetto* (scenario), or *commedia all'improviso.* The latter terms suggest something unlearned and unfinished. It is worthwhile to emphasize that it was not unlearned and, though unfinished on paper, it was completed on the stage. A study of the extant scenarios impresses us that the plays had finished plots and in that respect were as artful and well made as, and very like, the *commedia erudita* of Ariosto, the comedy of Molière, or that of Goldoni. They are not vaudeville sketches or witless farces but fully developed comedies. *Commedia erudita,* after all, was usually made in the same way—the plot first. There is a story of a playwright congratulating himself on a certain day because he had just completed a comedy. Now all he had to do was write the dialogue. Plot was the first and important thing in "wrighting"; then came prose dialogue, and last of all, verse, if that embellishment was wanted. We note the dependence on academic convention of the literary dramatists and are inclined to think antithetically of commedia as independent of literature. But literary elements were part of the improvised dialogue. The resources of Latin comedy and contemporary writing were used. *Commedia erudita* was looted for what it was worth and given slangy, snappy revision. The audacious surmise of the professional comedians that in the bright moment they could do better than the careful scholar in patient contemplation was at least a workable premise for them. Most often they improvised comedy, but tragedy, historical melodramas, and pastoral romances are also among the 600 scenarios that have been preserved.

The scenarios provided a scene by scene résumé of the plot, the scene unit being conceived of as starting with the entrance or exit of a character. The action and the points to be developed in the scene were noted briefly. The improvisation could not be a matter of free fancy but had to be done with an alert regard for the plot. Otherwise, some matter might have been enlarged or neglected or might have veered off in a direction that would have wrecked the plot. At rehearsals the action was planned so that certain entrances and exits would be used consistently. Details of the scenario were reviewed so that no contradiction would slip in if it were important to fix the time and place of a scene. Since disguise, mistaken identity, misapprehension, and comic irony were exploited fully in the plots, no performer could afford to be careless of his place in the scheme. The improviser was at the mercy of his partner's wits and neither could be dull or preoccupied. A successful effort was the work of the ensemble, each member being aware of his own limits and alert to the quirks, method, and mood of the others. All members had to be mindful of the situation and of what came before and after. In this they differed from many of the improvisers we see today. The brilliant Jonathan Winters, for example, makes his improvisations comparatively brief. The commedia player had to

keep on the track of the plot for three acts.

A typical commedia company might have had ten players. Two Old Men, two zanni or servant clowns, and a Captain were usually masked characters. The remaining five were most often "straight" characters and were not masked. There were two pairs of lovers, *amorosi,* and a serving slut or maid.

Each stock character was developed by its performer, the actor or actress playing the same role or mask in every play. The actor who played Pantalone, for example, specialized in the role throughout his career. If a performer changed his role and developed a new one, such a change marked a new phase of his career; the new role became his speciality from then on. This practice made improvisation easier to develop because ordinarily one role was given a lifetime of study and practice and was developed as the actor's personality and experience suggested. Any actor will agree that it is easiest to improvise a role he knows well. Because the actor played his own creation, because the role was his familiar spirit, the wellsprings of thought and emotion were easily reached and did not need to be tapped by the exquisite apparatus of a Stanislavski method. The sixteenth-century actor had an opportunity to build a role that is usually denied a modern actor, who seldom returns to the same role. In a way, the player of this one role, always building on his earlier work in the role, may have imbued his acting with a stylization and polish that in itself was something to see.

This system might be expected to make the stock characters appear the same in play after play. Several things worked against that tendency. The role was varied by the demands of each new plot. In some scenarios the Pantalone would be grave and sober, a man of some substance. In another he might be a horny old fool enamored of a courtesan, with the life of the role lying in its senile hunger for Eve's flesh. The name was the same, but the game was not the same and a rather different character was played. In theatre parlance, the roles were in the same "line" but not of the same "type." A second circumstance served to vary the playing of the role; it was set off by its presentation with the assorted other characters in the company. The Pantalone who confided in the Doctor was not the same man who took Arlecchino or the Captain aside. The various masks were sharply contrasted because there was a particular value to be obtained if they were. Laurel and Hardy were both fools but different kinds of fools, and the flavor of their fooling gained by the difference. It may be getting down to very fine points to suggest a third lever that would move the actor to vary his attack. An improvising ensemble responded sensitively to any change in personnel. The quality of a new Arlecchino elicited new reactions from the Pantalone. Their relationship necessarily adjusted and varied.

Because an improvising actor is dependent on his partner, he may well be more carefully aware of him. This heightened awareness is at the bottom of rich, full acting. The actors in sixteenth-century commedia were not players of many parts. It was not their business to act—as the supreme actor of all time, Sir Laurence Olivier, has acted—a tragic king, a fop, an impetuous warrior, a senile squire, and an introspective doctor at various performances in a single repertory week. But if we cannot say they were versatile in that sense, we may say their success hints at resilience and variety and suggests they did not spend their days on stage doing the same thing over and over again.

The masks used in commedia dell'arte covered the brow, eyes, nose, and cheeks. Made of leather and lined with linen, they were small enough to free the mouth but large enough to caricature the features:

the brow, nose, and cheeks were broadly modeled and made fantastic. Masks have something potent in them; they are never as dead as we who have a theatre without them suppose. We do not laugh, we are not cruel when the heavens fall on an ordinary mortal, John Doe's pratfalls do not amuse us; but give us some sign that another kind of being is before us, whether the sign be a clown face, a dead pan, a rigid pose, or a subhuman mask, and we develop an appetite, a disposition to see extravagant behavior and even disaster as comic. A mask stirs expectations based on our familiarity with it, and clowns and comedians know this. They come to count on the introduction the sign or mask provides. "In playing comedy," the old boys say, "a bit of red should be applied to the nose."

Masks affect the performer, too. Some of the spirit that shapes a mask and limns its features enters the wearer, as witness the behavior of a Halloween child in a false face. It would be difficult to set down a concrete statement regarding the effect of masks on the players of commedia. I am convinced the effect was real; a masked man is no ordinary mortal. A less nebulous effect of masks is that they imbue an actor with a quite lively sense that his body and voice must be used more eloquently. Indeed, there is an art to playing with a mask, and its chief ingredient is bodily expression. When his face and eyes can convey nothing, the actor, sensing the loss, compensates by a more expressive use of posture, movement, and gesture. He uses his voice in a richer way with a fuller range and more varied tempo. It is like the effect of laryngitis on an actor. He discovers his body is never so eloquent as when his voice loses some of its tones and expressiveness. So, if he can bestow nothing with his glance, the actor plays his part by demonstrating his other resources. The masked commedia performers were noted for their superb pantomime and gesture. Their success in foreign lands, where their dialogue denoted little, must have been due to the rich connotations they conveyed by what we call body language, by their great skill at using varied tones of voice, tempi, and expressive gestures and movements.

A notably popular feature of their performances was the acting of night scenes. In sunshine or on the well-lit court stage, they gave the illusion of playing in darkness by creating with carefully mimed movement the character's apprehension of what he could not see, deriving plot turns and comedy from the mistakes of a night. The creation of night by mime is a notable feature of the Japanese Kabuki actor's repertoire of technical display. There it dates from a time, as with commedia, when mime was the only way to play a night scene. Recently, Peter Shaffer's engaging farce *Black Comedy* pulled this stunt from the actor's bag and audiences delighted in the charade: on a well-lit stage the performers behaved as though they were in the dark.

Having set down these observations on the playing, we will now take up the individual masks. The two Old Men of Italian comedy were Pantalone and the Doctor, who often bore the name Gratiano. They were usually paired in the plays as fathers, husbands, old fools in love, or counselors. The first has Shakespeare's phrase "the lean and slipper'd Pantaloon" to bring part of the mask to mind. Another part of the mask is suggested by his title of *Il Magnifico,* a side of the character as often displayed by the performers of the role. Pantalone was usually a Venetian merchant, as his red vest, breeches, and long black coat declared. His mask had a hooked nose and he wore a pointed beard. At times the plot presented him as a cuckold or duped parent, as ridiculous in love, tricked by his zanni servants, or lapsed in the antics of

querulous age. But he could also be serious, a counselor rather than a tedious scold. His companion came from Bologna, then as now a university town. Gratiano was a learned doctor rather than a medico. He dressed in black, in contrast with Pantalone's red. His nose was bulbous compared to Pantalone's lean. His academic gown and cap signaled the contents of his head and the phrasing of his garrulous tongue. He brought saws and instances, Latin phrases, names, dates, the whole windy convolutions of learning with a capital "L," to buttress platitudes. The humor of his discourse lay in its malapropisms, its contrast between sound and substance, its meandering obscurity, and its everlasting extent. Polonius as counselor in Act II, scene 2 of *Hamlet* has more than a touch of the Doctor. A source of comedy for the Doctor's role was his credulousness and his incompetence in ordinary affairs. There have always been those who are amused and satisfied when they find out the professor is a bumbling boob who doesn't know everything. Better when he knows nothing and discusses it.

Another mask was the Captain. Italy in the sixteenth century had its unfair share of foreign conquerors, and the swaggerer predictably appeared in commedia. There was a vein of comedy to be mined in presenting a Spanish soldier as a braggart who was a coward, a fierce soldier who talked grandiloquently and ran at the first sign of a fight. A mocking portrayal of a soldier also yielded something like a redress of grievances, as it burst the bubble reputation. Some of the Captain's blood flows in Plautus' *Miles Gloriosus* and in Shakespeare's Parolles and Pistol. *Il Capitano* was as pretentious as his cape and sword, as fantastic as his moustaches and plumed hat. He vaunted his learning as well as his valor, using stunning rhetoric to impose an image of his near relationship to fabled heroes and legendary worthies. His wacky, mad hyperbole embraced monsters, titans, and gods. He told marvelous, incredible tales and if his servant was perplexed and did not know which ones to believe, the Captain could reassure him: "Believe whichever you please, Trappola mine." The Captain could be a hyperbolic lover as well as a fool drunk with his own glory, and then some of Mercutio's fancy or the panache of Cyrano would come to him.

The zanni were the clowns of commedia with more of realism than circus clowns. They were like the plotting slaves of Roman comedy but with a freer wit and a more generous dash of impertinence. Individual players gave their own slant to the roles, and with at least two zanni in most plots they shaped their playing to contrast with the other zanni of the company. Thus there might be a droll stupidity in one and a trickster's wit in another. Goldoni's *Servant of Two Masters* and Molière's *Scapin* present literary examples of the two types. Abbott and Costello exemplify the contrast as well. Another trick in performance was to contrast the servant with his master, to set off a bumbling or hoodwinked Pantalone or Doctor with a clever servant, to set off sophistication with peasant wit, city air with country breeze, Don Quixote with Sancho Panza. The humble servant often burlesqued the fashionable manners and speech of his betters. The zanni were not minor characters relegated to a subplot, as are the clowns of Shakespearean drama. They often bore the leading roles; in their nimble or numb natures lay the mainspring of many a plot's complexities.

Zany, Zanni or Zan is the name of an early clown. His name may confuse the reader, for it became the generic term for the whole group of zanni (it has been so used above). His name could also denote the commedia itself, as in "Zany's come-

FIG. 17. Zanni *by Jacques Callot. Francatrippe was the mask of Gabrielle Panzanini da Bologna, who was the* zany *with the* Gelosi. *A famous Bolognese clown of the next generation was Pier Maria Cecchini (1587–1622) who acted with the* Accesi *and played Fritellino. He was a contemporary, and at times fretful, colleague of Giambattista Andreini. Theatre Arts Prints.*

dies"; the dressing room provided for a commedia troupe in a Florentine court theatre was labeled zanni's room. Zany was at first the top banana of the group of frisky servants. Early pictures show him in loose trousers and blouse, wearing a brimmed hat adorned with impertinent feathers. He has a knife too large for comfort tucked in his belt and often plays a stringed instrument, the *vielle* or Italian lyre. His mask gives him a droll above-it-all look of amusement. In picture and scenario Zany is Pantalone's servant, carrying his letters, instructing him in wooing or in serenade, and standing behind his master enjoying the incongruous confrontations he has brought on.

Arlecchino, whom we know as Harlequin, became the most famous of all the zanni, indeed the most famous of all the masks. At first the second servant, he ended as *the* commedia clown. Originally from Bergamo, a hill town marking the extent of Venetian territory, Arlecchino was an innocent country fellow, amoral and good-natured, inclined to greed and always hungry. He was a rascal without malice. The troubles of such a character are the result of his eager grasp of the moment, of one thing at a time, in a world that expects more of its children and demands more of its servants. This role was played variously as its great exponents developed it to suit their own talents, but most often there was an emphasis on nimble light-foot movement and acrobatics. Arlecchino's trousers and jacket were close-fitting, as is appropriate for a dancing figure. His patched clothes and the rabbit tail on his small cap bespoke his country origin. Later, the patches were stylishly metamorphosed into a bright, multicolored theatrical pattern. His black mask was a hairy, wrinkled, snub-nosed thing with pin eyes.

Besides Arlecchino, many other types of clowns appeared. Many of their natures are not as distinct as their names. Coviello, Scapino, and Brighella seem to have been portrayed as clever scamps adept at living by their wits. Brighella is often thought of as the partner of Arlecchino (the Abbott to his Costello). He was also from Bergamo, was a rougher sort, tricky, and less to be trusted than his fellow Bergamask. Brighella's mask was olive and his nose crooked. Coviello, from Naples, was probably a contrast to another more famous Neapolitan, Pulchinella, who was mercurial: he clucked vacuously or displayed a barbed wit, was inclined to be vulgar, mean, and stupid, but also had a vein of understanding generosity. Pulchinella had a hook nose, protruding stomach, and humped back. He was costumed in loose white trousers, shirt, and peaked cap. Some scholars have asked if his prototype was Dossennus, the humpback of Atellan farce. Others see Maccus as his prototype. In time Pulchinella became Punch, the terrible-tempered Mr. Bang of Punch and Judy puppet shows. Pedrolino, another zanni, was a sometime

faithful servant and patient man who became the born loser; his heir is the sentimental white-faced clown we know as Pierrot.

In improvising this passel of eccentrics, the performers exploited the provincial and dialect humor that went with their masks. Neapolitans, Bergamasks, and Venetians jostled and jibed at one another in their distinctive ways. We know something of these eccentrics from vaudeville and radio entertainers who were impolite enough to wring comedy from the broken English and oddities of minority groups. The late Fred Allen, in "Allen's Alley", had a collection of characters that included the dour Yankee Titus Moody, the convivial Mrs. Nussbaum, and the declarative Southern gasbag, Senator Claghorn. A commedia show brought its stewing plot to a mad boil of fitful Old Men, Captains, and zanni and added the salt tang of their Italian regional peculiarities.

An unknown philosopher has wisely said, "Fun's fun but no girl wants to laugh all the time." The balance of a more sensible center, a saner reference point, was provided by the lovers. They were comedians, too, but the commedia had—in addition to the eccentricities and crudities of deportment, dress, and speech of the exhuberant ones—the graceful carriage and manners, the rich fashionable dress, and the polished Tuscan of the refined and well-spoken *amorosi*. Many of the performers of these roles were literary artists whose poems, letters, and dramas were published and praised. Their improvisation was replete with figures of speech, stichomythia, couplet tags, and an impressive array of rhetorical devices which were part of the educated discourse of the time. The *amorosi* had class. The premeditated art of their polished passages, or *concetti*, was published as model expressions of despairs, laments, accusations, dec-

Harlequin.   Zany Corneto.   Il Segnor Pantalon.

O la belle chanfon, Pantalon chantons bien, | Accordons nous tous trois, fi bien & proprement | Courage (mes amis) ie chante le deffus,
Si voulez efgayer voftre maiftreffe belle, | Que puiffions l'endormir au doux fon de ma lire, | De ce plaifant trio, compofé pour madame,
C'eft le moyen certain pour en fin iouir d'elle, | Encor que comme vous ie n'aye apris à lire, | La douceur de ma voix luy penetrera l'ame:
Qu'eftre mufeau de chien, dy-ie muficien. | Ie ne laifferay pas de iouer brauement. | Mes paffages ne font ni tortus ni boffus.   j.

FIG. 18. *Engraving of a serenade scene from an early commedia dell'arte.* (*From Beijer's* Fragments des Premières Comedies des Italiennes.) *Theatre Arts Prints.*

larations of love, and explorations of subtle feeling. Their fancy dialogues had the theatricalism of operatic duets and set pieces.

The very names of the *amorosi* bespeak the glamour of the roles. Lelio, Orazio, and Flavio sound like the leading men they were. Isabella, Silvia, Vittoria, and Flaminia are names that conjure feminine beauty, grace, and spirit. With these charming ones on the boards, commedia dell'arte beguiled the Italian comic stage of a curious stricture. Before, no women had prominent roles. Heroines like Progne, Orbecche, Canace, and others of their ilk were suffered to dwell in the horror and blood

bathos of tragedy, and nymphs and shepherdesses dwelt in the happier, rarer atmosphere of pastoral plays. But in *commedia erudita,* as in Roman comedy, women had a very modest share in the action. A tradition as hoary as a time when no admirable girl ventured abroad accounts for their comparative absence from the traffic of the classic scene of a public street. An interior scene, where a nice girl would keep herself, seemed as hard to imagine or come by as a chaste maid in the open air; neither had any classic precedent. So nurse companions were trotted out as go-betweens. Servants profited from the trade in messages that took the place of confrontations. Passions came secondhand. There was probably more hearsay evidence than should be admitted in drama. Some heroines in comedy who had been lost in childhood or had been stolen by pirates purchased with their misfortune a license to appear in the street. For girls who were lost and did not know who they were could gad about without a chaperone until they learned who they were and became (near the end of the comedy) as demure as their good-girl status required. With admired artifice the playwright deployed rings, pendants, birthmarks, and moles (or some such identifying sign his poor heroine was ignorant of) to bring about the moment of recognition when all losses are restored and sorrows end. A happy ending is no less happy for being contrived, and commedia dell'arte did not throw out plot claptrap. But it did bring on the girls in an unashamed display of lovers confronting one another. The *amorose* came on stage to propose, refuse, adore, detest, protest, sass, quarrel, forgive, and gambol with their men. They were the pioneers of a full portrayal of comic heroines on the European stage.

Comedy before and after commedia has used bawds and gusty women servants, and so, of course, did commedia. This mask, named Franceschina or Smeraldina, was played by an actor at times. Probably those times came when the maidservant role was that of an older woman who was more nasty than gracious. A less crude maid was performed by actresses. Sometimes they consorted with the zanni and sometimes they served the *amorose* as companions or confidants. Later there developed a pert serving girl, who in some scenarios had the leading role. A petite, vivacious lass named Arlecchina or Colombina appeared.

NOTES

Fynes Morison, quoted in the headnote, was an English traveler in Italy (1617). K. M. Lea's *Italian Popular Comedy* is the source of the comment (p. 343) and of much of the material in this chapter.

Other major sources are Nicoll's *Development, Masks,* and *Harlequin,* the Smith works, and Oreglia's study. Other useful books on commedia are listed in the bibliography; their titles reveal their pertinent content.

Lea provides the Coleridge lecture note (p. 359) and quotes Petrarch on Bambasio (p. 35); the intriguing farce title is taken from Herrick's *Italian Comedy* (p. 43); Ganassa at the banquet in Ferrara is mentioned in Lea, p. 252; Nicoll records the objection to "unnatural tomblinge" on p. 304 of his *Masks;* Smith's *Italian Actors* records the Bolognese complaint about "Zani's Comedies" (p. 26); Nagler's *Sourcebook* (p. 261) quotes Coryat on Venetian mountebanks; the Avignon commedia shows are described in Wiley (p. 26), where Martinelli's impertinence to Henry IV is also set down (p. 23); Arlecchino's familiarity with Marie de Medici is given on p. 279 of Nicoll's *Masks,* and his *World of Harlequin* (p. 33) tells of the performers "always reading, always gathering . . ."; Lea quotes Spavento, "Believe whichever you please, Trappola mine" on p. 44.

Chapter VI

COMMEDIA DELL'ARTE, TROUPES AND PLAYERS

Scaramuccia non parla, e dice gran cose
—EVARISTO GHERARDI

Commedia dell'arte continued as a vigorous form of theatre well into the eighteenth century. The springtime of its life in the last quarter of the sixteenth century was a hectic one. The name of the form does not translate as tonily as "art" but rather as skill or professional comedy. This comedy of the professionals was done by players necessarily organized as traveling troupes, the first sizable groups of professional actors in modern Europe. Their pioneering attempt to be their own masters, to perform year-round, to earn their way from a paying public (in certain lucky seasons from the patronage of prelate and prince), their very attempt to be independently professional was hardy, even foolhardy, and their success is a testament to their artistry and skill. A public used to the free theatre of church festivals or the irregular luxury of ducal dramatic display was not in the habit of giving a mite to a vagabond, however talented or entertaining. No patron had any notion of being obliged to a player for his services beyond an immediate occasion. And so the professionals had to play when, where, with, and for whom they could. Their history is hard to trace and harder to treat, for the records we have merely outline a confusing chronicle. It is a tangle of short-lived combinations, squabbles, failures, pleas, patronage, bold venturing, triumph, and defeat.

The most famous and best of the professional companies was the *Gelosi,* which can be traced from about 1570 to 1604. The name advertised their zeal to please, that they were "The Jealous of Pleasing Ones." No other company had so steady an identity nor a group of performers who were as highly regarded. They played in public in Venice and other Italian cities and appeared frequently at the courts of Ferrara and Mantua. They made several extended visits to France, playing at Lyons and Paris. At the French court they enjoyed the patronage of Catherine de'Medici, the widowed Queen of Henry II and mother of the last Valois kings. Catherine de'Medici welcomed them for the delight of hearing her native Italian and for their professional artistry, which easily surpassed any French company of the sixteenth century.

The *Gelosi* came to France for the first time in 1571. After a successful series of performances at court, they ventured to Paris where their plays were criticized as teaching "adultery" and serving as "a school of debauchery to the youth of both sexes." Except that it is some evidence of the players' Parisian presence, the criticism need not be taken seriously. There must have been native teachers of the mysteries objected to and places of instruction more efficacious than a public stage. If the objection does describe the curriculum, we are comforted by the notice that it was coeducational. The *Gelosi* had considerably more to recommend it, however. Two years later at Ferrara the company appeared in the premiere performance of the most charming of pastoral plays, Tasso's *Aminta*. It was a splendid courtly occasion directed by the poet himself and unlikely to have been entrusted to a heavy-handed bunch of lewd players.

In 1574 the French king, Henry III, journeying from Poland to his crown in France after the death of Charles IX, saw the *Gelosi* perform at Venice and was especially delighted with them. In the company at the time was Giulio Pasquate, who was renowned as the first brilliant Pantalone. Also in the company then was a superb Zany, Simone da Bologna. Three years later Henry invited the *Gelosi* to play for him at Blois, and they spent the summer of 1577 performing at the Hotel de Bourbon in Paris. They attracted such a "concourse and crowd of spectators that the four best preachers of Paris, all together, did not gather so many." Was the quality of the pulpit not up to standard, was the populace unusually frivolous that summer, or were the crowds lured by a surpassing group of entertainers? Most likely the *Gelosi* had become a troupe with the skill to present a varied repertoire that could sustain an audience's interest over a long summer. They played in Paris from May to September.

The next year, 1578, there were two artists in the *Gelosi* of extraordinary talent. The first was Francesco Andreini, a 30-year-old ex-soldier who had spent eight years as a captive of the Turks. He was an accomplished linguist and writer who first appeared as an *amoroso* and then developed the role of the most celebrated commedia Captain, Capitano Spavento de Vall'Inferno. The word *spavento* may be translated as "terror."

In 1607, after he had retired from the stage, Andreini published his popular *Bra-*

FIG. 19. *Isabella Andreini. An engraving by A. Locatelli after the portrait engraved by Raphael Sadeler. From* Enter the Actress *by Rosamond Gilder, published by Theatre Arts Books.*

vure del Capitano Spavento, a collection of his dialogues with his servant, Trappola. The flavor of the fantastic Captain and his creator's wit is preserved in such bits as this one, in which he vaunts his birth: It was not like any other. He was not born "nude and puling" but clad in armor, "roaring like an impatient lion and hissing like an enraged serpent." Bemused by his own vision of that memorable day, the Captain makes no comment to Trappola's guess that his "mother's womb suffered mightily from such a strange conception." There had been no warm bath, no swaddling bands, no pap for the hyperbolic tyke. "I as soon as I was born, was washed in molten lead, clad in red-hot iron, and fed with hemlock . . . and deadly nightshade." Andreini's rich imagination set the Captain's role on the roaring road it was to take.

The other newcomer to the *Gelosi* in 1578 was Isabella Canali, a 16-year-old beauty who became Andreini's wife the same year. Isabella Andreini became the foremost commedia actress, the *prima donna inamorata*. To her contemporaries Isabella seemed, in her husband's words, *"bella di nome, bella di corpo, e bellissima d'animo."* One wrote of her as the "ornament of the stage, a proud spectacle of virtue no less than of beauty, who has so adorned her profession . . . every voice will echo her famous name."

Soon the Andreini became the effective leaders of the *Gelosi.* It was a sign of their prestige that in 1589, when the grand duke of Tuscany, Ferdinando I, married Christina of Lorraine and the most lavish of celebrations was planned, the *Gelosi* was invited to give two performances in Florence. One of the plays presented was Isabella's starring vehicle, *La Pazzia.* The play was a series of feigned and "real" mad scenes for its heroine, and Isabella played them with

brilliant effect. In 1603 the company returned to France and appeared before Marie de'Medici and Henry IV at Fontainebleau. The *Gelosi* lingered at court for more than a month and then played in Paris from the end of that year until April of the next. On the journey back to Italy, Isabella died unexpectedly at Lyons. A public funeral was given, a surprising tribute for an actress in that day. Her epitaph noted her "preeminent" virtue and that "the chief of theatrical artists" there awaited the resurrection. Her loving husband, Francesco, quit the stage and the *Gelosi* disbanded that spring of 1604.

Isabella not only shared the hardships of her husband's profession and became a superb comedienne, she also bore seven children and developed a literary talent which was highly regarded. Her four daughters entered Mantuan convents; one son be-

FIG. 20. *A commedia dell'arte troupe in a painting at the* Musée Carnavalet, *Paris. It is likely the troupe portrayed is the* Gelosi *and the charming* amorosa *is Isabella. The kneeling figure may be Francesco Andreini; the Pantalone, Giulio Pasquati; and the smirking* zany, *the Francatrippe of Gabrielle Panzanini. The Francheschina with the* Gelosi *was Silvia Roncagli.*

came a monk and another became a soldier in the Mantuan service. The Andreini's eldest son, Giambattista, became an outstanding commedia player, manager, and writer of scenarios and plays. As an author, Isabella was honored as a *laureata* of the Paduan *Accademia degli'Intenti,* and she was ranked with Tasso and Petrarch. Critics of our day would not rank her so high, but her contemporaries esteemed her pastoral play *Mirtilla,* and her *Lettere* had six printings in the half-century after her death.

The less notable commedia companies did not have as happy or continuous a history as the *Gelosi.* Although the *Gelosi* was successful, its existence was not a succession of carefree journeys. One of the troupe's best patrons was the Mantuan court, and the *Gelosi* are sometimes referred to as a Mantuan troupe. Two anecdotes of how the company fared there throw a dismaying light on the relations of the commedia performers with their arbitrary patrons. In 1579 a particular comedy was prepared by the *Gelosi* at the behest of the duke. Mightily pleased at the result, the duke asked who had been the author, and in expectation of a plenteous reward, three players responded at once. The Zany, Pantalone, and Gratiano each claimed credit, whereupon the duke, now mighty displeased, imprisoned and tortured the trio. In 1582 three of the troupe (we hope not the same three) offended the duke in some way by their performance. They were commanded to walk a tightrope. The rope broke and the consequence of this rude trial was that they fell straight into prison. As on the earlier occasion, the very lives of the hapless players were in danger. The dungeon of a Renaissance prince was no place to be, and the usual term was for life. No wonder that the next year Francesco Andreini declined an invitation to come to Mantua, preferring to stay with the *Gelosi* in Venice.

In such circumstances a company's association with a particular court was rather fortuitous. The existence and membership of most companies depended on who got along with whom. Drusiano Martinelli, an enterprising player-manager who made successful tours to England and Spain, was cherished by the duke of Mantua for the sake of his wife, Angelica. It seems the duke cherished Angelica as much or more for her private graciousness as for her public performance. In his solicitations to the duke, Martinelli referred to himself as the husband of Madonna Angelica, which may have been the politest title he could give himself. For a time Drusiano Martinelli led a famous company called the *Uniti,* but a history of such a company is suspect for it seems to have been a name bestowed on various troupe combinations.

The various mentions of one of the most famous of early *amorose,* Diana Ponti, give us a picture of the volatile nature of the troupes. Diana Ponti's steadiest identification is as her mask, Lavinia. In terms of company relationship, her career was a crazy quilt. She was at one time the leader of the *Desiosi* ("The Desirous of Pleasing Ones"), a company having little history beyond its link with Diana Ponti. During the twenty-three years before 1605 in which historians say she flourished, Diana also was with the *Confidenti,* the *Uniti* (whatever that might have meant in 1586), and the *Accessi* ("The Brilliant Ones").

A sometime leader of the *Accessi* was Tristano Martinelli, the first great, if not the first, Arlecchino. Tristano enjoyed a greater reputation than his brother, Drusiano. Perhaps because he ardently sought his own preferment, this Martinelli was not as delightful to his co-workers as he was to his public and patrons. He did not appear for long in any one company. Marie de'Medici enjoyed him a great deal; he called her "Dear Gossip" and frequented France. His wit and wheedling is preserved in his 1601 publication, *Compositions de rhetorique de M. Don Arlequin*. Tristano Martinelli made a lot of money.

Besides the Andreini, another famous couple in commedia's early years was Giovanni Pellesini and Vittoria Piissimi. Pellesini played Pedrolino until his death in 1612, when he was close to 90 years old. For a time this most famous Pedrolino acted with the *Gelosi*. He may have been the Pedrolino who inhabited the banquet pie at Ferrara in 1582. About that time he may have married Vittoria Piissimi, for he became closely associated with her in the leadership of the troupe called the *Confidenti* ("The Confident Ones"). Vittoria played Fioretta, a serving girl, and also performed in her own name as an *amorosa*. As Vittoria she was Isabella's chief rival. Described as a "beautiful witch of love . . . with harmonious and pleasing speech, accomplished and graceful actions," she had both "sugared smiles" and "a carriage haughty and noble." The *Confidenti* troupe had a reputation second only to the *Gelosi*.

Flaminio Scala was the leader of a second company that bore the name *Confidenti*. Scala appeared as Flavio with the *Gelosi*, the *Uniti* (1598 edition), and the *Accessi* before he became director of the second *Confidenti* about 1610. After that he may have been chiefly a manager. The author of many scenarios, Scala published a valued collection in 1611 which gives us our earliest evidence of the commedia repertoire.

Giambattista Andreini was a second-generation star who carried on the tradition and excellent reputation of his family. His *Fedeli* company inherited the mantle of the *Gelosi* and was patronized by the courts of Mantua, Ferrara, and France. As Lelio, he played opposite his first wife, Virginia Ramponi, a charming singer who appeared as Florinda, and his second wife, Virginia Rotari, who played Lidia. Andreini earned a reputation not only as the leading player

and the head of his outstanding troupe but also as a writer of tragedy, sacred plays, comedies, and pastoral romances. He ended his long life out of favor with his patrons and ignored, the rather pathetic figure of an actor worn out in service and wanted no more.

Surviving letters of the time indicate that the early commedia troupes were beset with spectacular jealousies and quarrels—that the performers had trouble getting along with one another. In this form of theatre, success greatly depended on sweet harmony, and professional rivalry, covetousness, and hanky-panky were doubly unfortunate. They were part of the player's life and added to the distress and disorder of his constant travels and his anxious relations with his patrons. Not every actress was as virtuous as Isabella, and some leering louts have ascribed some of the troupes' troubles to the bother women can be. They are ungenerous and nasty to say so; magnanimity would not make that report. The Englishman Thomas Nashe, in his *Pierce Pennilesse*, compared the London actors at the end of the sixteenth century to those "beyond sea," describing them as "a sort of squirting baudie Comedians, that have Whores & common Curtizans to play womens partes, & forbeare no immodest speech, or unchast action that may procure laughter." We may assume this was not so with the boys of London, who played the women's roles there. The report of a true traveler, Thomas Coryat, at Venice in 1608, is of another mind: "Here I observed certaine things that I never saw before. For I saw women acte . . . and they performed it with as good a grace, action, gesture, and whatsoever convenient for a Player, as ever I saw any masculine Actor."

Nashe extolled the honorable "representations" of his native stage where kings and princes appeared "full of gallant resolution," contrasting it with the lesser theatre of

FIG. 21. *A Baroque commedia dell'arte.* (*From* Monumenta Scenica.) *Hanswurst, a German mask of immense popularity, is here joined with Arlequin in a scene in which both are dismissed and scolded by Pantalone. The incipient Katzenjammer Kid up center, a gloating, gluttonous figure, is identified in the caption as Pierot. Theatre Arts Prints.*

"Pantaloun, a Whore, & a Zanie." We ask ourselves if this was all that commedia dell'arte amounted to. We must admit that at times commedia may well have been no more, but as our narrative has shown, it often was a great deal more. Had it not, it would not have successfully occupied the European stage and continued very alive through two centuries. In seventeenth-century Paris commedia troupes existed side by side with Molière and influenced both his acting and his writing. The masks and fooleries continued in the dramatic texts of Molière, Marivaux, and Goldoni. They became immortal figures. In France the commedia planted a tradition of mime performance exemplified in our own day by Jean-Louis Barrault and Marcel Marceau.

Commedia has a persistent attraction for all who love theatre and its central art of acting. It belonged so clearly to the performer. It did not need dramatists; none was available. It did not need scenic claptrap and clutter. In the courts commedia made use of those expensive superfluities. But more often, we imagine, the performer mounted a rude open-air platform with a curtain at the back to mark an offstage area. Perhaps this cloth behind him had a paint or charcoal indication of locale, a well-painted perspective decoration, or maybe some rude architectural scribble. We think of this performer as limited to his own resources and the impedimenta a patient mule might carry on the road from one town to another. Bored with a theatre that "transports" us to parlors, street corners, and alleys and tells us, "By their cups and saucers, their lamp posts, and their trash cans ye shall know them," we forget that these supposedly real things—these bits of crockery, posts, and cans—are only as real as wax fruit unless the actor makes them real. If an actor plays a lucky man who finds a million bucks, what difference can it make if he comes upon genuine currency, five-and-dime play money, a prop man's unreasonable facsimile, or thin air? We do not pose the question and so we are ready to applaud the brave performer who accepts the challenge to work with "three boards and a passion." We applaud the vision of the commedia performer's acceptance of that challenge. Those players came on with the minimum of the actor's bright costume and the maximum of skill to bedeck the boards with their verbal wizardry, their acrobatic tricks, their songs and dances, to create a memorable art knowing no bounds of country or of tongue. If at times the actress in breeches parading about town to drum up a muster did not draw a happy throng to their booth, if sometimes the costumes were shabby, the wit was halting, the turns did

not come off, if the magic of their music and their nimble motion did not succeed, if sometimes it rained, the commedia remains an ideal and in that realm the skies are bright, the tricks and turns wring delight, and we are not sober.

We study theatre history to recreate in imagination the old forms of theatre. As we do this academic penance, imposed for our neglect of our theatrical heritage, we envy the Japanese who have absolution because they have managed to preserve their old forms in living performance. If only we had been as careful, particularly when it comes to a form like commedia that is so slippery and elusive! We penitents may hope, as we look at the pictures so vigorously alive in posture and pose, as we study costume and mask, scenarios and contemporary descriptions. And how lively that hope becomes when we see a recreation on stage, like the superb Arlecchino of the late Marcello Moretti of the *Piccolo Teatro* of Milan and see him seconded by a brilliant company playing to a strongly marked rhythmic beat that crackles and thunders its own exuberance. And then, on second thought, we realize that for all our piety, our piled up details of how it was, commedia will not quite come alive that way because it belongs to the performer and must begin with him.

There is another road to take. The clowns of our own day and our enjoyment of them is a better study, not because they are descendants of commedia but because in themselves they can help us see it. Buster Keaton, Bert Lahr, and Charlie Chaplin tell it like it is and like it was. Robert Morse in *How to Succeed in Business Without Really Trying* can tell us in terms of our time what Arlecchino was up to and in his quite different way so can the late Cliff Arquette in the mask of Charley Weaver. Out in the Midwest, the tent-show Toby and Susy carry on. Flip Wilson gives us the flash and dash of the zanni up against it and around it with

FIG. 22. *Commedia dell'arte figures by Jacques Callot. Razullo appears to be a zany and Cucurucu a Captain. Callot is apt to dress his Captain figures a bit shabbily. In the background of these hard-to-identify masks stands a booth stage. From Mantzius'* A History of Theatrical Art.

FIG. 23. *This seventeenth-century Dutch commedia dell'-arte, from a painting by Troost, presents Harlequin as a barber. Theatre Arts Prints.*

his wits. The list could lengthen but we come to the point: all of these performers, so individual, so much their own kinds of fools, will not lend their capers to a copyist. Commedia begins with and belongs to the performer who brings his life to the mask.

NOTES

The greatest of seventeenth-century actors was Tiberio Fiorilli, an Italian who enchanted his Parisian public as Scaramouche. This note is a tribute to his art penned by the Harlequin of the same troupe of Italian comedians in Paris.

To the works listed as major sources for Chapter V add, for this chapter, Gilder's *Enter the Actress.*

See page 28 of Smith's *Italian Actors* for the account of the *Gelosi*'s first Parisian run, p. 306 of Nicoll's *Masks* for the quote about their outdrawing the Parisian pulpit, p. 249 of the same work for Spavento's *Bravure,* and p. 237 for the tribute to Isabella. The description of her as the "ornament of the stage" and her epitaph are quoted by Smith (pp. 47 and 52). Vittoria is described in Smith, p. 46. Thomas Nashe's words about commedia can be found on pp. 90–91 of the edition of *Pierce Penni-lesse,* published by E. P. Dutton & Co., New York, 1924. Coryat's observations are given in Nagler's *Sourcebook,* p. 259.

Chapter VII

THE PASTORAL

*If we present a Pastoral, we show the harmless
love of Shepherds diversely moralized, dis-
tinguishing betwixt the craft of the city, and
the innocence of the Sheep-coat.*

—THOMAS HEYWOOD

In the first half of the sixteenth century the Italians began a revival of Roman dramatic art; at least they wanted to think so and, their wishes fathering the thought, they tended to think they had. If wishes were horses, beggars would ride. And if their dramatic activities had had an abrupt end in the year 1550, we might agree they had put together a pocket edition of the classic theatre. Although the bumptious commedia dell'arte had just begun to march to its own tune, the amphitheatres the Italians had set up in front of the pretty prospect of the Serlian stage, the kinds of plays they took most seriously, and their dramatic criticism and studies before 1550 proceeded to the measures of a pavane for a dead princess, the Classic Muse. If that were all, we might agree. But the history of their work is longer and these descendants of Rome did more.

In the hundred years following the mid-century year of 1550 the Italians realized theatre forms implied by their work of the century before but not yet created. After 1550 came pastoral plays and opera. Both of these were newly made, although it could be argued that they, too, derived from Roman devotions. In the same hundred-year period after 1550, the Italians developed scenic techniques that changed the shape of European theatre. Since then the theatre of the West has been uniquely Italian in its physical shape; if we were to define it with one modifier, the best and truest name we can give it is the Italian Stage. An ordinary desk dictionary pictures a stage and neatly charts the location and shape of the proscenium, wings, borders, and backdrop—stage contraptions first regularly used by the Italians. Our idea that a stage is more than an acting platform is Italian. Our idea that a stage setting should locate the action, should go with a particular scene or play, came to us from Italy. From Italy we learned to expect a single glance at the stage to give us a picture organized as a whole, just as we take in a painting organized by perspective. There the stage was first set to create a unified picture. There after 1550 were devised the ways to change that picture as the locale of the drama changed, and from this came the fundamental and whimsical notion that the stage picture should change. Although today we have our theoretical quarrels with naturalism and realistic illusion, although our theatre has been changing in this century, and although we are less rigid in our expectation that our stage should be a picture stage, we habitually think of the stage in the Italian way. We have been doing so for more than four centuries. In this we are the heirs of the Renaissance Italians, not the heirs of antique or medieval or Elizabethan habits. They persuaded us to think of the stage as a place for changeable pictures as well as acting, a place for architects, painters, and machinists as well as actors.

After the seemingly sudden appearance of commedia dell'arte, the first new development of the second half of the sixteenth century was the pastoral play. This kind of play had its roots in the disputes of canny shepherds in the eclogue (read, recited, and then acted) and in the mythological plays and entertainments of the *Favola d'Orfeo* ilk. The pastoral play was the creation of the court at Ferrara; Ercole II and then Alfonso II and Cardinal Luigi d'Este were its patrons. Just as the earlier generation had sponsored the translation of Roman comedy and Ariosto's *commedia erudita,* this generation encouraged Cinthio's tragedy and the new pastoral plays of Beccari, Argenti, Tasso, and Guarini. Guarini was himself a descendent of the humanist teacher who first came to Ferrara a century before.

Agostino Beccari was, in the words of this new Guarini, the first "to possess the happy boldness to make in this kind." In 1554 Beccarri's *Sacrifizio* was presented before duke and cardinal. With its three pairs of lovers, it was a drama combining something of pastoral poetry, classic myth, and an essential and pretentious longing for an innocence and a simplicity supposedly nurtured and effulgent in the breasts of shepherds and shepherdesses whose habitat is hills and vales. Their wood notes sounded again at Ferrara in 1567 in Agostino Argenti's *Lo Sfortunato*. The author of the masterpiece in this form, Torquato Tasso, was in the audience.

Six years later, in 1573, Tasso's *Aminta* was presented in the Belvedere, an Este pleasure island in the Po River, performed by the *Gelosi*. Tasso sang of Aminta's loving before he knew what loving was, of his love for the "careless" Silvia, of how he rescued

FIG. 24. *The Italian comedians in Paris.* (*Gherardi's* Théâtre Italien, *1741.*) Esope *was played in 1691. As in many of the plays produced by the Italian troupe in Paris, Arlequin appears in strange garb and with strange companions. The setting is appropriate for a pastoral romance. Theatre Arts Prints.*

her from a satyr, how she fled and was reported killed while hunting, of how Aminta went off to commit suicide when he heard of her supposed death, of how Silvia returned from the hunt and took the news of Aminta's supposed death, and of how their odds were made even with kisses. *Aminta* had more than 200 printings in Italian and was widely translated. It stands as the superlative poem in pastoral drama, inimitable in its charm and gentle harmonious flow.

The second impressive play of this special genre was Giovan Battista Guarini's *Il Pastor fido,* completed about 1586 but not produced until later in the next decade. It was longer and more complex in plot than Tasso's *Aminta.* The objections made to Guarini's play by the pedants of the time measure the pastoral's audacious movement into the realm where tragedy and comedy mix, where some classic rules are in abeyance, where Guarini and his predecessors in pastoral were asserting that poetry came before rule.

Marlowe's lyric sounds the invitation of the pastoral play:

The shepherd's swains shall dance and sing
For thy delight each May morning.
If these delights thy mind may move
Then live with me and be my love.

© The Duke of Devonshire.

FIG. 25. *This design is labeled "Pastoral sceane Som: House, 1625." Somerset House was the residence of 16-year-old Queen Henrietta Marie, who arrived in England early in the summer of 1625. On Shrove Tuesday of the next year, the queen and her ladies (some of whom wore false whiskers to play the male roles) performed the French pastoral play* Artenice. *Englishmen unused to the very idea of women acting were shocked that a queen should do it, even in her home. The idea, of course, seemed not at all startling to the young queen, who was the daughter of Marie de Medici. Inigo Jones' setting is, in the main, satyric in the Serlian sense of the word, but to the left are elements reminiscent of Serlio's comedy scene, and, on the right, of the tragic scene. Perhaps we may consider this design a reflection of the critical fuss made over pastoral plays—that they were not decently one thing or another but a mixed form. This is one of several scenes used in the production of* Artenice, *which was the first play to use changeable scenery (as distinct from a Masque) at the English court. Theatre Arts Prints.*

These shepherds are not disputing or talking of their betters, as in an eclogue. These dear happy groves of Arcadia are lit by the gentle rays of morn and evening; satyrs and storms do no harm there. Raleigh's conditional acceptance, "Had joys no date, nor age no need," reminds us that the pastoral's appeal is to a poignant, indulgent melancholy. The concept that from sylvan springs flows surcease from sorrow, that mountains are medicinal is a product of jaded appetites. The world grows old "and growing old, grows sad." The pastoral was escapist, no more bold nor buoyant than the suspicious air of the Counter-Reformation could bear. In creating the pastoral play, the Italians enriched the theatre with a sweet strain of music, a strain that echoed in Elizabethan lyrics and in some Jacobean plays. It gave stage space to a sweeter love and to lovers unlike those in boisterous comedy, unlike those in the grim tragedies of the time.

NOTES

Heywood's *Apology* (1612) is the source for this chapter's headnote.

Material in this chapter had its source in Greg's *Pastoral Poetry & Pastoral Drama*. In Cheney's *The Theatre*, there is a brief and helpful appreciation. Daphne's speech about the world "growing old" from *Aminta* is quoted from Leigh Hunt's translation, Act II, scene 2.

THE ROMAN RELIC AT VICENZA

Palladio wanting to leave behind him a work of art of perfect workmanship persuaded these academicians . . . to construct a theatre according to the ancient use of the Greeks and Romans.

—FILIPPO PIGAFETTO

In 1556 an aristocratic circle of classical enthusiasts founded the Olympic Academy at Vicenza, near Venice. Their hobby included the staging of plays (classic and neoclassic) which they did in temporarily erected theatres. Among them was the great architect Andrea Palladio. In 1580 he began the realization of a Vitruvian dream he shared with his fellow academicians, the design and construction of a proper theatre cut to the Roman model. Past 70 when the work began, Palladio died the same year. Four years later the architect's masterpiece was completed by his son.

On March 3, 1585, a select and impressed audience of gentlefolk that included the Empress Maria of Austria, the French ambassador, and Venetian nobles saw a production of Sophocles' *Oedipus* at the inaugural of the *Teatro Olimpico*. No less a critic than Aristotle had given the play his special praise, and it seemed to the audience that they were seeing the greatest play of all in the greatest theatre of all. So wrote one of them who praised the effect of the choral music, the perfume in the air (used to simulate the incense wafted from the altars of stricken Thebes), the eighty expensive costumes (gold cloth for the king and queen), the well-spoken unison chorus of fifteen, the

two dozen Turkishly dressed archers who were part of Oedipus' entourage, and the conspicuous retinues of Jocasta and Creon. But what was most admired was the theatre and stage itself.

On that March afternoon in 1585, the audience came early to enjoy the building. The fourscore academicians were proud hosts who accommodated 400 noble ladies in the orchestra section of their new amphitheatre and served their audience wine and fruit. The auditorium, placed within a wide rectangle about 100 by 45 feet, had a rather steep amphitheatre with its thirteen rows arranged in a semiellipse. The flat orchestra below the first row and a portico above the last row curved in the same graceful ellipse. Statues of the academicians were placed atop the portico and in niches in its center and on the extreme ends. Palladio had given the theatre splendid proportions, and when he chose an elliptical arrangement rather than the semicircular arcs of Vitruvius and Serlio he brought his audience closer to the stage, improved the sight lines, and gave his auditorium a pleasant intimacy. At about 7:30 in the evening, the perfumed air of the theatre was rent with the sound of drums and trumpets and the explosion of firecrackers, and a curtain fell, revealing the archi-

FIG. 26. *The* Teatro Olimpico, *Vicenza, as it appears today.*

tectural splendor of the stage. The stage was an area about 80 feet wide and 20 feet deep backed by an elaborate scenic facade, adorned with statues, columns, and reliefs, and pierced by five doorways. With a large central archway and two flanking doors facing the audience, and with two lesser doorways set at right angles to the auditorium at the extreme ends of the facade, the Olympic Academy had handsomely re-created the Roman stage.

Behind, upstage of the five doorways, was a scenic contraption that smacked more of Serlio than Vitruvius. It was the work of another architect, Vincenzo Scamozzi. On the raked floor behind, upstage of the facade, Scamozzi placed perspective vistas behind each opening. Three streets converged in the vista behind the central archway and single streets carried the eye off into the distance behind the other four open doorways. The vanishing point of each vista was nicely calculated at an angle which gave everyone in the elliptical auditorium a good view of the enchanting depth to be seen by looking down at least one perspective alley. The whole arrangement suggested a splendid city square with seven streets radiating from it. (There had been seven principal streets in the Thebes of Greek tragedy.) The street vistas were built of wooden angle wings and

the "buildings" were adorned with statues (flat cutout boards skillfully painted) and architectural features. Some years later the great English architect and stage designer Inigo Jones, master of the King's Works under James I and Charles I, described Palladio's theatre with these words: "The perspectives are five . . . with houses, temples and such like. In front at the end of the scene an arch triumphal . . . the chief artifice was that where so ever you sat you saw one of these prospects." Scamozzi's chief artifice, the thing that struck Jones' practiced eye, was, of course, that behind Palladio's scenic facade the usual Serlian setting had been multiplied by the employment of seven vanishing points. It had been laid out in order to bestow the pleasures of perspective on the whole audience, not just (as was usually the case) on the small number who could crowd about a duke so as to view it from seats near a point directly opposite the one central vanishing point. This has been explained as stemming from the fact that the academicians were a fraternal group of aristocrats, no one of them important enough to outrank the others as others were outranked at court. Compared with the usual perspective, Scamozzi's five pros-

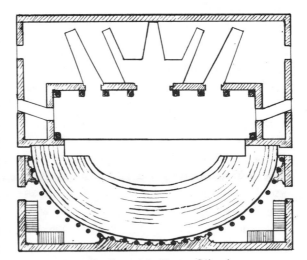

FIG. 27. *Plan of the* Teatro Olimpico.

pects seemed to carry off to a greater distance. The space used for them was actually quite deep, and each vista was viewed through a doorway that served as a proscenium for it. The Palladian theatre with the Scamozzi vistas still stands, a picture postcard subject, and four centuries worth of travelers to Vicenza have been impressed with its beauty and proportions.

Some scholars have supposed Palladio may have originally planned to back the doorways of his stage with *periaktoi*. Had he done so, he would have followed one Renaissance interpretation of an intriguing paragraph from Vitruvius. In describing the *scaena,* or scenic facade, the Roman wrote:

> In the center are double doors decorated like those of a royal palace. At the right and left are the doors of the guest chambers. Beyond are spaces provided for decoration —places that the Greeks call *periaktoi,* because in these places are triangular pieces of machinery which revolve, each having three decorated faces. When the play is to be changed, or when gods enter to the accompaniment of sudden claps of thunder, these may be revolved and present a face differently decorated. Beyond these places are the projecting wings which afford entrances to the stage, one from the forum, the other from abroad.

The first two and last sentences, which order the placement of the five doors of the facade, are the easy ones. What they describe was done at Vicenza. It is the muddy middle of the paragraph that is puzzling. What is meant by "beyond"—behind or farther off? We do not know. When we guess, we have difficulty reconciling our understanding of *periaktoi* with the demands effective entrances and sight lines impose on the use of stage space. Some students of Vitruvius' text (and perhaps Palladio was one of them) guess that "triangular pieces of machinery

which revolve" should be placed in the doorways of the facade. Such an interpretation is shown in a plan of a Roman theatre published by Daniello Barbaro (Palladio's friend and fellow worker) a few years before the theatre at Vicenza was built. Whatever Palladio's intention, Scamozzi's vistas were more "modern," expressing Renaissance rather than Roman theatre practice and giving the *Olimpico* the best of both worlds.

Some writers of theatre history have interpreted the great central doorway of the *Olimpico* facade, which Inigo Jones saw as an "arch triumphal," as the modern proscenium arch in embryo. By some evolutionary analogy, they see the *Olimpico* arch growing greater, broadening to open up the scenic facade, and moving downstage toward the audience in a time lapse series of steps to become the great frame of what they consider the later picture stage. The Palladian central doorway is the archetypical arch. This thought has its attractions for prophets of progress who cherish in their hearts a desire to give Palladio's brilliant and beautiful architecture some sort of status as a harbinger of things to come. But the proscenium as we know it existed well before 1585 in the temporary court theatres of Italy and even earlier in the stages erected for entry displays. Palladio's stage can only be called a throwback, if a name for it must be found in the vocabulary of those who are preoccupied with biological concepts. How neat it would be if the perspective stage described by Serlio had not come first, for then Serlio's seemingly more modern stage could be classified as evolving from Scamozzi's pretty vistas. But the facts will not let us be neat. It is a fact that Palladio's Roman relic was built in the 1580's, long after Italian architects had left the Roman scenic facade out of the picture for the sake of the brighter prospect of the Serlian street scene. So Roman a theatre as the *Olimpico* was not built

FIG. 28. *Stage of the* Teatro Olimpico. *Courtesy The Metropolitan Museum of Art. Harris Brisbane Dick Fund, 1942.*

later in Europe. And in this same decade of the 1580's so "modern" a stage as the one Serlio described, a stage represented at Vicenza by Scamozzi's vistas, was to be supplanted by a stage with a novelty behind the proscenium arch, a novelty called changeable scenery. This is matter for our next chapter.

The Olympic Academy achieved what it wanted, a Vitruvian theatre for classic revivals, a theatre that was an antique before it was made, a wave not of the future but of the past. It does not belittle the work of Palladio and Scamozzi to say that other, stronger tides were shaping theatre architecture and stage design and that in view of those tides this occasion we have described was a last hurrah for classic devotions. The proper salute to the *Teatro Olimpico* is, therefore, the old Roman *"ave atque vale."*

On odd Tuesdays, however, when we are whimsical enough to consider what might have been, we say farewell wistfully. What if the stage of our Western world had continued to be architectural rather than scenic? What if being "Italian" meant Italian in the way represented by Vicenza rather than Italian, as it is, in the way represented by Florence? What if Palladio, rather than the artists who created changeable scenery, had been our stage's forefather? Our stage would then have been unlocalized, unscenic, a decorative rather than a representational thing, as it had been for Shakespeare. Our plays might have continued to have the sweep and scope and quickness that an unlocalized stage encourages and that a scenic stage can only permit at considerable bother and expense. It would mean that modern producers, working with our scenic stage and having to submit to its demands, would not ask our playwrights to save bother and expense by providing a one-set show. It would mean that modern plays which eschew the eye-catching trickery of scenic illusion, such as those of Bertolt Brecht, and that modern theatres which are handsomely architectural rather than scenic, such as that at the Shakespeare Festival of Stratford, Ontario, would not seem so new. It would mean that these latest things would be old hat.

In 1958 a German director wrote a letter which may be prophetic. "The picture frame stage," he wrote, "will . . . one day disappear again. And it is to theatre buildings from the Earliest Times up to the Renaissance—including the delectable Teatro Olimpico—that we must turn to build after in terms of modern methods." If this idea is correct, the *Teatro Olimpico* may be a wave of the future after all.

NOTES

The head quote was written in 1585 by a spectator at Vicenza for the premiere performance. It is part of a letter which provides basic material for this chapter. It is given in Nagler's *Sourcebook* (pp. 81–86) and in Kernodle's *From Art to Theatre* (p. 169). Kernodle "sees" the *Olimpico* a bit differently, and the reader may wish to find out about that by looking at his Chapter V.

The way Inigo Jones saw the *Olimpico* is taken from Campbell, p. 56. Vitruvius on *periaktoi* can be found on p. 150 of the edition of Morgan (see notes to Chapter IV of this book). The letter quoted at the end of this chapter was taken from p. 208 of Southern, *The Seven Ages of the Theatre*.

Nicoll's *Development* was an additional source for this chapter.

Chapter IX

FLORENTINE INTERMEZZI AND CHANGEABLE SCENERY

Sometimes as many as seven changes of scene are built at no little expense. Especially in Italy . . . as much as a half ton of gold has been spent for a play that would have only one performance at a princely celebration. . . .
—JOSEPH FURTTENBACH

The tide shaping the Italian, and thus the European, stage was in the late sixteenth century moving toward its flood at the court of the grand duke of Tuscany in Florence. Eleven months after the curtain fell at Vicenza (a century after Duke Ercole's courtyard staging of *Menaechmi* at Ferrara) the *Teatro Medici* had its first production. The occasion, the theatre, and the entertainment were all unlike those at Vicenza.

The theatre in Florence that had its premiere performance on February 6, 1586, was called into being by the second grand duke of Tuscany, Francesco de'Medici, whose father, Cosimo I, had wrought a small, strong kingdom, unrivaled in Italy, and had gained for himself and his heirs the sweet fruition of an earthly crown. Under Cosimo, Florence had prospered and grown to a population of 80,000. The *Teatro Medici,* like some prestigious crown jewel, was to be the outward and visible sign of Medicean magnificence, a memorable display for the princely visitors who would come to Florence for the wedding of Virginia de'Medici to the Ferrarese Cesare d'Este. It is no part of theatre history that the bride, Virginia de'Medici, was the daughter of Camilla Martelli and Cosimo I (born before Cosimo made Camilla his second wife); that the reigning grand duke, Cosimo's heir, Francesco, had no affection

for Camilla Martelli, the bride's mother; that he packed her off to a convent after his father died and let her out on only this occasion. These circumstances make it difficult to explain the opening of the *Teatro Medici* as the product of a simple desire to celebrate the marriage of Grand Duke Francesco's half-sister. The Tuscan grand duke was interested in illusions of grandeur, and the marriage linking this *nouveau* branch of the Medici to the Este of older repute was an occasion for indulgence. For this event, Francesco de'Medici was not his usual self—a dour duke who exercised a careful economy.

Two remarkable men were on hand to give the duke what he wanted. One was Count Giovanni de'Bardi, who is remembered as the author of comedies, the planner of intermezzi, and the rich, talented patron-leader of the Florentine circle that created opera. Bardi conducted careful rehearsals of the comedy to be performed, his own *L'Amico fido,* and its concomitant confectionary, the intermezzi. He also devised the themes for the intermezzi and composed music for the final intermezzo. The second man was an ingenious, capable, inventive architect and fireworks expert, Bernardo Buontalenti. The theatre and stage, its machinery and settings, were his responsibility. The scope of the artifice mustered to serve the grand duke on this conspicuous occasion

81.

is indicated by the fact that Buontalenti, in his capacity as what we call technical director, directed the work of 400 men.

In a great hall in the Uffizi Palace, Buontalenti set up a stage about 9 feet high and 38 feet deep; the width of the stage and the hall was 67 feet, and the audience occupied a long rectangular space, 144 by 67 feet, with a richly decorated ceiling 46 feet above the floor. A dais was raised in the center of the hall for the guests of highest rank; around it the floor was sloped so that the gentlemen seated there could have a clear view of the stage, and along the side walls of the hall and the far wall opposite the stage were six carpeted banks of steps for the ladies. A gallery above these side wall seats was topped with a leafy trellis where blossoms winked. Birds and woodland creatures peeped among the foliage. The hall must have been brilliantly lit, for it was decorated with metallic pyramids bearing lighted urns and column tops bearing lighted gilt baskets. Suspended from the ceiling were sixteen chandeliers shaped of six harpy creatures, all of them bearing torches. There were skillful simulations of expensive ornamentation: fountains, festoons, statues of pagan gods, boys, and babies. As the guests came into the midst of this abundant artifice, birds were released from baskets, their chirping flight adding to the din of courtier chatter which probably was as admiring as the duke desired.

It is hard to imagine a pedant so hung up on his visions of antiquity, so demure, as to bring sobriety to that luxuriance. However, it may be worthwhile to entertain the idea of such a person. He may have been there; perhaps he was a Venetian who had been to Vicenza the year before. The Grand Duke Francesco's consort was Bianca Capello, a Titian-tressed beauty from Venice. Venetian emissaries were in attendance at Florence and a pedant may have been in their midst. Such an imaginary one may

have thought to himself that Buontalenti had it all wrong. This auditorium was not classic. It had nothing of Vitruvius' circular base; this was a blatant rectangle. And the placement of the ducal dais was a sure sign that when the rich, red drapery revealed the stage perspective it would turn out to have one vanishing point dead center appearing to be about 60 feet away from the curtain line. (Our pedant would have guessed 60 feet because the grand duke's dais was set at that distance from the stage.) They had managed the amphitheatre layout more correctly at Vicenza, he might have thought, for Palladio's elliptical departure from Vitruvius' circle was not as radical as these right-angled banks of seats along the walls in this boxy excuse for a theatre. At Vicenza they had managed to be more democratic (though our pedant would not have used the word), for at the *Teatro Olimpico* "where so ever you sat" you could see a coherent perspective picture.

When the curtain lowered, "the most lovely views and most peculiar buildings and squares" of Florence appeared. From chimneys arose perfumed smoke, perhaps reminding our pedant of the Theban incense he had sniffed from the stage at the start of *Oedipus*. What other odors assailed his lean nose or what appeal Bardi's *L'Amico fido* made to his understanding that night in the Uffizi does not concern us. And probably pedantry was lost in wonder at the delights the grand duke's architect had made. The long night's dreams were those of music for the ear, spectacular visions for the eye, and the most astounding feats of engineering for the mind to ponder in amazement.

The intermezzi began before the comedy and dominated the entertainment. In the sky over the stage setting of Florentine streets and buildings made to serve the comedy appeared a cloud bearing great Jove himself, who enriched the dawning day by sending Virtues as blessings for the nuptials. The cloud discharged its freight and disappeared "without anyone being able to see how its various portions vanished." The fabulous, cloud-born figures included ten gods and ten Virtues presented in splendid costume with splendid music. All of this was an aerial prologue to the comedy, the heavens above opening to show this first intermezzo. Then followed Act One of Bardi's comedy. After the first act there was a startling, rapid, and complete change in the stage picture, managed (as were such things then) in full view of the audience. Lo, Florence, the realm of *L'Amico fido,* and lo, an immense cavern and in the distance the city of Dis in flame and smoke, Furies on flaming towers, and all the evils of the world banished to this hell. This second intermezzo's locale and personages emphasized by contrast the theme of nuptial rejoicing. On such a day Virtues come to earth from heaven, as in the prologue intermezzo, and Evils go to hell, as in this vivid inferno—flying machines for one and trap work for the other. This fearsome second realm vanished as magically as it came and the Florentine street reappeared for the second act of the comedy. Then a third intermezzo began with another complete change of picture. A bare landscape appeared which itself changed to become a vernal delight when sweetly ministered to by Flora, zephyr *"con altre festevoli deità, amoretti, aure, ninfe e satiri."* Trees put forth their blossoms and foliage as in the lyric, "Where'er you walk, cool gales shall fan the glade, trees where you sit shall crowd into a shade." After the third act of the comedy, another complete change replaced the Florentine vista. Again, note the relationship of intermezzi episodes achieved by contrast. The preceding scene had been of stricken land and now there was a storm-tossed sea with cliffs and rocks, a waterfall, monsters rampant, and ships in distress. Then Thetis, tritons, and the horse-drawn chariot of Neptune brought homage

and all was pacific. For the fifth intermezzo Buontalenti kept the Florentine setting in view and deployed the sky machinery, sending a lovely cloud to dispel thunder, lightning, and darkness. And in that cloud appeared a chariot (drawn by peacocks who spread their tails) carrying Juno, who bore felicitations. Rain and rainbow appeared. Again the cloud disappeared and no one knew how. Finally, after the comedy's fifth act, there was another complete change of scene to the countryside. On a flowery plain with trees, a grotto, a palace, and animals, Tuscan shepherds and shepherdesses danced and sang. They were, of course, beings as mythological and musical as any that had trod the boards, rode the traps, or flew the sky apparatus that night.

I cannot tell how the comedy fared that interrupted this pageantry. There had been two intermezzi marvels of cloud work in the heavens above the mock Florence on the Uffizi stage below and four complete changes of scene embracing hell, earth, sea, and Tuscan pastures. Nor can I tell how the new Medici bride and the Este groom fared with so many benisons purchased at such a rate. After this show and others like it, the theatre fared differently. How Buontalenti made his changes, how he animated his machinery in 1586, we do not know precisely. He clearly had the good talent his name proclaims and he may have invented a remarkable number of the devices he needed, or he may have used and improved those of earlier scenic artists. His cloud machines seemed more miraculous, his scene changes more frequent and more swiftly accomplished, than any ever seen before. The life he gave Neptune's horses and Juno's peacocks seemed, as the saying goes, real. Buontalenti was clearly a virtuoso at mechanical contrivance and in the employment of changeable scenery, and he may have been the first to use changeable scenery regularly in staging intermezzi. To say the

FIG. 29. *The* Teatro Medici, *Florence, by Jacques Callot. This shows the Uffizi hall as it appeared in 1617 when it was fit up by Giulio Parigi for the production of* La Liberazione di Tirreno e d'Arnea. *The first intermezzo of the show featured a ballet of twelve men who were joined in the cleared floor of the auditorium by twelve ladies. The Grand Duke Cosimo II and his consort were among those performing. The largeness of the theatre is apparent, and the horseshoe-shaped auditorium of later opera houses seems to be prefigured here. The curved ramps connecting stage and auditorium space are a bit unusual, but designers of this time thought of stage and auditorium as one space and did not trouble themselves with our modern notion of a "fourth wall." Sometimes the curtain which hid the scene before the start of the entertainment was painted to "go with" the decor of the hall. Sometimes the parapet or low wall in front of the stage had painted stairways or doors "connecting" platform and auditorium (see figures 7, 12, and 25). From* Theatre Festivals of the Medici *1539–1647 by A. M. Nagler, published by Yale University Press.*

least, this production marked the arrival of changeable scenery on the court stage. No rival princes could suffer the Tuscan duke to possess alone the plum of admiration such a toy was designed to harvest. They were covetous enough to send word to their architects to conjure productions like Buontalenti's at Florence. They conjured, and conjuring gave our theatre an expensive facet.

We have some notion from the story thus far of why our theatre came to use scenery rather than mere decoration. With this Florentine extravaganza in mind, we want to learn something of how and why scenery became changeable. But first we digress to consider some matters of theory related to changeable scenery and certain aspects of the intermezzi.

Changeable scenery had its theoretical basis in notes surviving from Vitruvius and other classical writers, intriguing snippets that made up for their brief imprecision by their antiquity. Vitruvius' note about the *periaktoi,* "When the play is to be changed, or when gods enter . . . these may be revolved and present a face differently decorated," suggests alternation for an intermezzo which met both qualifications as to when the *periaktoi* were to be revolved. The intermezzi were a realm apart; it would follow that they might "present a face differently decorated." A note by Philander provided in his commentary on Vitruvius in 1544 described not only the *scena versatilis* (or *periaktoi*) but also another method of scene change called the *scena ductilis,* "by which, through panels drawn to the side, this or that scene is revealed within." Philander's note gave a theoretical warrant for the flat wings and shutters which were to develop later and replace the two-faced, angle wings of Serlian stage design. How much bearing theoretical notes of this sort had on the practical matter of mounting a court show is a good question.

Quite apart from matters of theory, it seems that the observance of unity of place in the early plays might have made it inevitable that the variation the intermezzi provided would come to be a cherished part of any court production. That, as they say, is show business. Once intermezzi were established, they in turn encouraged the development of machines, scenic apparatus, and eventually changeable scenery. It also seems more certain that changeable scenery was needed and came to be when the intermezzi shows became more than entr'acte diversions and became the place for politic congratulations—when they became populated with the conspicuously courteous pagan gods and mythological creatures, those supernatural ambassadors who came to bless the deeds of dukes and furbish their reputations. The more prosaic people of neo-Plautine comedy could not accomplish this mission. Nor would it seem that intermezzi creatures could do much better than comedians if they set about their mission while on the city street of the usual comic scene. Would it not seem that scenes and machines whose product was wonder should be called into being by this mission? Would not the image, the full stage pictorial embodiment of these beings, seem truer than a poet's wordy invocation? Flying clouds and chariots are needed to bring on the gods. And the more complete the vision, the more fully, the more wonderfully, the truer, the whole spectacle presented this vision. It would seem that in order to do what they were required to do the intermezzi would have had to use changeable scenery. However, as we shall see, there was not quite so direct a relationship. Intermezzi were ever present after the act of a court play for nearly a century before changeable scenery appeared to improve their wonder.

The development of changeable scenery can best be illustrated by looking at records of productions at Florence. Other cities and courts made their contributions to this peculiar thing, but at Florence it was done as impressively as lavish expenditure could provide. Our outline begins nearly a half-century before the opening of the *Teatro Medici*. We backtrack to begin at the beginning and to stand on familiar ground before a court stage like the one described by Serlio. We go back to a time a few years before Serlio's architectural treatise appeared.

Cosimo I was elected "head of the Florentine Republic" at age 17 after the assassination of Alessandro de'Medici in January 1537. He came to power with not much chance of success, but he hung on in a remarkably effective way. He was on his way to becoming the grand duke of Tuscany and a new Augustus to the Florentines. It was noted that even his horoscope coincided with his Roman parallel. A first sign of his rise to status as a peer among the princes of Italy was his marriage after a little more than two years to Eleanora of Toledo.

And so in July 1539 the architect Bastiano da San Gallo, called Aristotile, decorated a courtyard and erected in it a stage for a comedy to celebrate the nuptials. The setting of the comedy was Pisa, and Vasari's description is of the usual Serlian thing. San Gallo's perspective was such that it would have been "impossible to assemble a greater variety of windows, doors, facades of palaces, streets and receding distances, all in perspective. He also represented the leaning tower, the cupola and round church of S. Giovanni, with other things of the city." Vasari cited admiringly an "ingenious wooden lantern, like an arch behind the buildings, and a sun . . . made of a crystal ball filled with distilled water, with . . . torches behind, illuminating the sky of the scenery and perspective . . . like a veritable sun." This lantern rose by means of a windlass into the eastern sky at the start of the comedy, inched to the apogee of its arc

at midpoint in the play, and descended at the end. Aside from this possibly novel touch, the production was typical of the court comedy settings in vogue for a generation. The setting did not change.

The intermezzi presented creatures unlikely to have appeared in the Pisa of the comedy, but they were creatures altogether usual and ordinarily expected in those interludes. They were rather nicely related to the time of day of the comedy and the progress of San Gallo's mobile sun. Thus the prologue featured Aurora combing her golden hair and singing while the sun rose behind her and dawn came to Pisa. The second interlude featured pastoral shepherds on the acting platform in front of the city streets. Another intermezzo was appropriately set by the Arno River, which flows past Pisa. San Gallo provided a simulation of the river in what Serlio was to label *"la piazza della scena"* in front of the stage. In this way anyone who wished for coherence of place, picture, and *personae* may have beheld with some satisfaction the intermezzo's three naked sirens if he supposed such exotic beings might swim in those waters. Appearing with the sirens were three sea-monster musicians and a trio of nymphs in transparent veils. The high noon intermezzo presented Silenus, and for him a set-piece grotto was plopped on the Pisan pavement. Did verisimilitude demand this scenic unit? As evening drew on, nymphs returned from the chase. At night bacchantes and satyrs cavorted on the stage.

Sustained by music, the show of these curiously costumed shepherds, nymphs, satyrs, and uncostumed sirens doubtless had a gratifying embodiment even though the background picture was a Pisan perspective. Did the music create another world where such beings existed? In part it did. But more surely their appearance satisfied expectation and when that is done, the oddest convention will never seem bizarre. This conven-

FIG. 30. *Three Sirens. These sirens were on display at the French Court in an elaborate and notable show of 1581. Engraving from Baltasar de Beaujoyeulx*, Le Balet Comique de la Reyne, *courtesy The Warburg Institute.*

tion may have been more readily accepted by the audience because it echoed the medieval stage convention that conceived of the stage platform as a neutral place that became a more definite locale only when the performers made it so by their relationship to a particular mansion or set piece in view. The grotto for Silenus may be thought of as a kind of mansion. When it was before the audience and a hung-over Silenus was in it, Pisa was nowhere, just as the Sea of Galilee of the Valenciennes stage was nowhere near the hell-mouth which was, in fact, beside it. To us it would seem that when the setting was rather general, when it was devised for a *type* of play (a religious play, a tragedy, a comedy, or a pastoral) rather than for a play with a unique locale, the setting might serve well enough as a backing for an intermezzo. But when greater verisimilitude was introduced, with details like the leaning tower of Pisa in this play, when the setting became more particular, it would seem less likely to serve the intermezzi. To our notion, the discrepancy between the play setting and the figures of the intermezzi would prompt the development

of changeable scenery, just as it may have prompted the grotto set piece for Silenus and the inclusion of the Arno River for the siren swimmers in San Gallo's view of Pisa. From San Gallo's day to Buontalenti's, there was a gradual, rather slow development of changeable scenery and while there was an increasing use of machinery to enhance the spectacle, there does not seem to have been a feeling that the intermezzi characters should be located in any particular place. Nor was there a feeling that they should be dislocated from the comedy scene.

It may be appropriate to cite a twentieth-century parallel. Our analogy is more instructive than exact. Neither in theme nor appearance do the pageants at the Tournament of Roses or the Orange Bowl relate to the football games they serve as intermezzi. No one enjoying such a spectacle wonders why it is there on the playing field.

Vasari recorded that Cosimo de'Medici was well pleased with his architect's work and that San Gallo provided him with settings for carnival time plays. San Gallo worked subsequently in Rome and at Castro, where in 1543 he used *periaktoi*. He may have been first to introduce them on the court stage. We know only the where and when of this innovation, not what he used it for or how.

There were several methods of shaping these prisms for a production. One method, perhaps the one used by San Gallo, employed triangular prisms having equilateral surfaces with one face of the three positioned to face the audience. Though this surface was flat, unlike angle wings, the architectural painting on the flat face was done in order to give the illusion of two visible sides of a building with one of the sides apparently diminishing as it would appear if it were actually angled toward the vanishing point of the scene. The *periaktoi* were not only painted to look like Serlian angle wings but they also were set up in the same way with several on each side of the stage. Upstage center, a larger *periaktoi* closed the gap between the two *periaktoi* farthest from the audience. The two faces of the triangular prisms that were out of sight could have had different decorations and been ready to revolve, bringing to view a different scene. The whole thing seems a clumsy way of building a scene and it is hard to imagine *periaktoi* becoming the basic unit of any scene unless the production used changeable scenery. In other words, why bother with these machines if not to change scene?

Another way of using *periaktoi* (we are guessing here) may have been to use a wedge-shaped device having three surfaces of unequal width rather than three of the same width. In plan, *periaktoi* of this type had an obtuse angle and two acute angles. Two of the surfaces of this three-sided machine (the two surfaces joined at an obtuse angle) made up a Serlian angle wing. The wider surface of the two served as the front face of that wing and the narrower surface served as the angled perspective face. The third side of this kind of *periaktoi* was the

widest of the three. The regular play's setting may have been painted on the two narrower surfaces and the remaining flat, widest surface when rotated into view bore the decor for the intermezzo. The less substantial realm of the dance interlude would then have been presented by more "artificial" painting on a flat surface. This flat surface would have been out of sight when the play setting was in view, and when out of sight its decor could have been changed and so prepared to bring on a different decoration or scene when the end of the act signaled the start of the next intermezzo. We must, however, set this down as something that could have happened. We do not know that it did. We know that some designers of the time used four-sided and polygonal *periaktoi* and that a century later the German designer Furttenbach drew a scheme employing wedge-shaped triangular machines which operated in pairs.

Periaktoi, in one form or another, are still with us. A recent Broadway production of Robert Bolt's *Vivat! Vivat, Regina!* used them to present the pageantry of the conflict of Elizabeth and Mary, Queen of Scots.

At Florence there was a continuing introduction of visual variation in production, but *periaktoi* and changeable scenes do not seem to have been used there until late in the 1560's. An interesting attempt at variety, made after San Gallo left Florence, is evidence that changeable scenery was not in use. At one end of a hall, Francesco Salviati provided the stage and decor for one comedy and at the other end, Angelo Bronzino provided stage and decor for another. Act One of one comedy was followed by Act One of the other, followed by Act Two of the first and so on, the acts of one comedy serving as intermezzi for the other. The audience obligingly turned from one to the other. We have here an example not of changeable scenery but of a changeable audience. It seems a nutty arrangement, but,

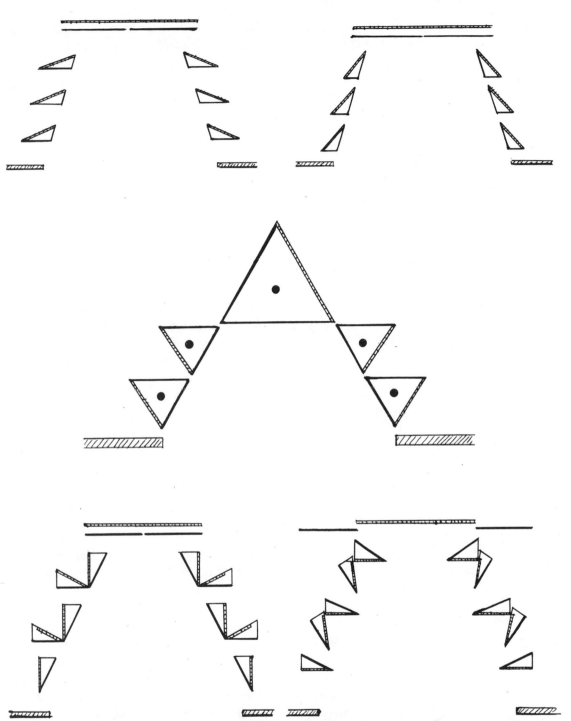

Fig. 31. *Four plans of scenes made of* periaktoi. *The larger scheme in the middle is that described and pictured by Ignazio Dante in his 1583 edition of Vignola's* Le Due regoli della prospective practica. *A clockwise rotation of the upstage center and the stage left machines, and a counterclockwise turn of the machines on stage right, brings a new scheme quickly to view. Above are two conjectural schemes showing how wedge-shaped* periaktoi *might be used to provide changeable scenery. The offstage flat surfaces in each scheme would bear a differently decorated scene. In each of these schemes, shutters are used upstage of the* periaktoi. *Below is a scheme taken from Joseph Furttenbach's* Architectura Recreationis *of 1640. It employs paired* periaktoi *and shutters upstage of them. On the left is shown their position for one scene. On the right, after a partial turn of each* periaktoi *and after the shutters are pulled offstage and out of sight, a different scene is in view.*

on the other hand, not so quaint if an inter-mezzo is customarily (not to say inevitably or invariably) presented after an act of a play. One wonders what has become of the vaunted value of unity of effect. Leone di Somi in his dialogues on stage matters ex-pressed the opinion, and it seems not to have been an opinion widely held, that the intermezzi often distracted from the plot of the play. No doubt they did. Who could mind a neoclassic plot, who could keep track of comic complexity when intermezzi allusions taxed their wits or visions of inter-mezzi nymphs danced in their heads? The usual costume for a nymph left her breasts bare. Less sensual types may have had their heads full of puzzles. To take an off-hand illustration, if Jason pursuing the golden fleece was the beloved duke, would the duchess be Medea?

In 1565 Cosimo I arranged the marriage of his son Francesco to Joanna of Austria. The bridegroom was even then enamored of Bianca Cappello and the new couple did not live happily ever after (Joanna died in 1578), but the marriage was an important confirmation of Cosimo's success and he at least rejoiced at the prospect of its consum-mation. Joanna was the daughter of the Hapsburg Emperor Ferdinand. This was to be the biggest and best show of Cosimo's reign and five months' preparation went into it. Events began with Joanna's entry into Florence in mid-December and con-tinued for two months. The festival comedy setting and decor of the hall in the Palazzo Vecchio were entrusted to the fine hand of Giorgio Vasari, whose Florentine comedy perspective scene served as background for the ubiquitous intermezzi. The intermezzi developed a coherent theme based on the story of Cupid and Psyche, and for them another artist provided elaborate cloud ma-chines and trap work. Apart from these di-verting feints managed by machines, there were no changeable scenes. Cupid and Psyche's intermezzo story was set in Flor-ence. The use of a single theme marks a development of the intermezzi to the point where they become no longer mere inter-ludes but the important feature of these court productions. In their allegorical way, of course, Cupid is Francesco and plain-Jane Joanna is Psyche. Practiced courtiers had no problem juggling ideas of that sort. The show was affective; it was recorded that Psyche's musical lament made the wedding guests cry. Maudlin moments, as much as merriment, make marriages.

Vasari was a more prodigal deviser when he arranged a posh procession for this 1565 marriage feast. He provided some twenty-one floats with as many statue-gods, which were attended by nearly 400 costumed fig-ures setting forth *La geneologia degli Dei de' gentili* in an esoteric, extravagant pa-rade of pagan gods and more than one would care to know of humanistic fine points about them, all key and symbol in the costuming and props. It is comforting to learn that after this pagan pageant dur-ing Lent that year of 1566, the Florentines mounted a special production of their tradi-tional Annunciation play in the church of Santo Spirito.

A definite record of changeable scenery at Florence followed soon after and is pro-vided by the records of two productions de-signed by Baldassare Lanci in 1568 and 1569. Lanci, a pupil of the esteemed Gi-rolamo Genga, entered the service of the Medici in 1561. At the end of the decade, he used *periaktoi* for scene changes in two carnival shows. The first show presented a Florentine setting which was covered by a cloud after the fourth act of the comedy. This cloud descended bearing the three Graces and the nine Muses. At the conclu-sion of their intermezzo, the cloud disap-peared and another view of Florence ap-peared. Here the comedy's fifth act was played. It is curious that this was a scene change for a play, not for an intermezzo. The next year, 1569, Lanci made a more completely different and earlier change of scene. Three acts of comedy and their intermezzi were set in Florence. Then there was a change to a country scene outside the city with a pond, cottages, and gardens displayed for the next intermezzi and for the last two acts of the comedy. Peasants danced in the first intermezzo following the change, and when they refused Leto a drink from the pond, magically, before the very eyes of the audience, these mean peasants were translated into frogs by means of ingenious costume design, the work of Bernardo Buontalenti. In myth no one was hospitable to Leto and the punishment may not have fit the crime, but it did earn Buontalenti his first notice in theatre history. This same country scene was used for the succeeding two acts of the comedy, which were set near the village of Arcetri. And so the succeeding intermezzi displays of Diana and her nymphs and of a gaggle of gods in the sky above had, at least to our way of thinking, appropriate backing.

Unfortunately for a seemingly logical theory that changeable scenery developed for the sake of the intermezzi, both of these productions, both using *periaktoi* and quite able to provide a change of scene, altered scenes for the sake of the comedy. The cloud scene used in the earlier production may have been brought on as much to conceal the scene change as to provide a distinct intermezzo realm. Thirty years before, San Gallo had made slight concession to the scenic needs of the intermezzi staged on the platform in front of a replica of Pisa. Why do more? Nymphs were expected to blossom on the unbosky street when the comedians deserted the platform at the end of an act. The 1565 festival intermezzi had a bit more visualization, with cloud machinery for heaven and trap work for hell. In 1568 Lanci set an intermezzo in

a complete cloud land. However, the way he used his *periaktoi* in 1569 demonstrated that, like San Gallo, Lanci did not think of a scene change as the inevitable thing when an intermezzo was planned.

Perhaps this careful inching toward changeable scenery need not be emphasized, except that that is the way it was—surprisingly slow. At some point intermezzi did become the occasion if not the reason for changeable scenery, and in 1586 at the premiere of the *Teatro Medici,* as has been noted, Buontalenti's four complete changes of scene were all done for the sake of the intermezzi. It was as though a flood of scenes and machines had spilled over a restraining dam of custom. Three years later this metaphorical dam burst and Buontalenti made seven completely different scenes, one scene for five acts of comedy and six for the six intermezzi.

In 1587 Francesco de'Medici died as much from the effect of partaking of the "immoderate embraces of his consort" as from his imbibing quantities of iced wine —as an irreverent contemporary who survived him thought. He was succeeded by another son of Cosimo I who doffed his cardinal's robes to become the third grand duke of Tuscany and to inaugurate a Tuscan golden age. This was Ferdinando de'Medici. In 1589 Ferdinando I a stately pleasure round decreed to celebrate his marriage to Christina of Lorraine. Entry, banquet, maypole erection, holy communion, high mass, tilting, jousting, reverence for a saint's relics, and a mule mangled by lions were parts of the parcel. Also in the three-week festival in May 1589 were big doings in the Medici theatre in the Uffizi. Indeed this theatrical festival provided the show of the century, surpassing all others. Work for it began in October of 1588. A comedy, *La Pellegrina,* was performed twice and two commedia plays by the *Gelosi* troupe were performed. On this occasion, Vittoria Piissimi acted with the *Gelosi*. Her starring vehicle, *La Zingara,* was presented on May 6 and was followed a week later by Isabella Andreini's *La Pazzia.* Apparently Vittoria suffered and Isabella succeeded in this confrontation of rivals. Both actresses had their work cut out for them. A minor bother was to make the plays conform to a Pisan setting provided for *La Pellegrina.* That comedy, acted by the *Intronati* academy of Siena, gentlemen jesters and esteemed performers though they were, would not have been as tough to follow as the intermezzi. The hallowed saw that there cannot be too much of a good thing was applied, and the intermezzi prepared to go with *La Pellegrina* were done with the commedia plays as well. The phrase "prepared to go with" is not apt, however, for the plays (both *erudita* and *improviso*) were quite incidental to the intermezzi, which were presented on four theatrical evenings.

An item of last-minute expense for these shows was the pay of a carpenter to provide practicable doors rather than painted simulations in the Pisan setting so that the actors could conveniently enter and exit. We pause to wonder if the audience could have been as aware of the performers in the plays as were the planners of this to-do.

The intermezzi were again based on themes wrought by Bardi and embodied by Buontalenti. Like San Gallo fifty years before him, Buontalenti had a Pisan street scene to provide for the comedy. Buontalenti in his bounty improved the prospect by showing a square with two streets: two vanishing points for him to calculate and for his audience to admire. On the intermezzi were bestowed a horde of pretty people and a prodigal display of scenic wizardry. For the first of these there was a prospect of Rome and goings-on in the heavens above. Thereafter, as the synopsis of scenes reveals, there were complete changes after each act: Pisa, garden scene,

Pisa, sylvan glade, Pisa, inferno, Pisa, seascape, Pisa, cloud scene. Two tailors with fifty assistants fussed and fit and ornamented nearly 300 costumes for the troupes of intermezzi creatures. Besides the principal mythic beings, there were attendant beauties, choruses, musicians, and dancers who supposedly put the audience in mind of a unifying theme—the influence of music in the lives of men. The first intermezzo treated the Doric mode, the most excellent; others dealt with a contest of Muses and Pierides, the Pythian songs of Delphi, disharmony (hell), the story of Orion (seascape), and Jupiter (in heaven) sending harmony, rhythm, and songs in honor of the present occasion—the wedding. The embroidery of the theme provides an embarrassment of riches to describe. Let five items be culled from the catalogue: a pasteboard Apollo in the sky who descended and was replaced by a "real" Apollo, who slew the Python, probably "fake"; a "fake" Lucifer big enough to eat children (over 15 feet tall) appearing in Inferno (two lucky Florentine kids had walk-on parts they surely remembered all their days); Amphitrite, nude in flesh-tone body stocking and jewels, towed on a shell through waves by perfume-squirting dolphins; Arion sang on the poop of a large galley, was attacked by sailors, was tossed into the sea, and was born away on a dolphin's back; and when the Muses won their contest in the second intermezzo, the Pierides changed to Magpies and rather large chattering birds left the scene (an echo of an earlier Buontalenti use of changeable costume).

Buontalenti's scene changes may have been managed by the use of wedge-shaped *periaktoi,* in which case two sides would have been set with the Pisan perspective and the third side with the intermezzi realms. Or, the changes may have been done with sliding flat wings, sliding on to cover the *periaktoi* that presented clouds and the

FIG. 32. *The first Intermezzo, 1589. This engraving by Caracci after Buontalenti shows the second of the two-part intermezzo,* The Harmony of the Spheres. *Far up in the heavens the six Virtues possessed by the Grand Duke Ferdinando I and Christina of Lorraine (Justice, Religion, Piety, Conjugal Love, Magnanimity, and Valor) are exemplified by a display of twelve heroes who had those good qualities in abundance. The dominant figure is Necessity, who appears with her spindle and is attended by three fates— one to sing of the past, one of the present, and one of the future. On the same level are the seven planets and the goddess of Justice, the herald of the Golden Age which is on the brink of beginning for Florence. These figures express the joy of the cosmos and are joined in this sentiment by the Sirens, who create the harmonious music of the spheres but have left their posts to take up positions on the lower, nearer clouds to praise Christina of Lorraine. For most of the audience, as for most of us, this cosmological meaning was lost in delight at a glimpse of paradise. It is interesting that, except for the female singer in the role of Necessity, all performers in this intermezzo were male, their female attributes furnished forth by papier mâché. From* Theatre Festivals of the Medici *1539–1647 by A. M. Nagler, published by Yale University Press.*

Pisan perspective. The latter possibility would give luster to Buontalenti's name, for it seems it was not until the early years of the seventeenth century that the flat wing system was generally in use. However done, Buontalenti had given the grand duke of Tuscany the show of the century.

This great Medici festival of 1589 set a pattern for court theatricals that was to last a long time. This pattern, which had been developing for a century, was to have plays, and soon operas, performed with change-able scenes, was to have intermezzi making the most of music, colorful costume, and ingenious machines to deal with royalty as though they were gods, and was to have the best performers of the best acting companies. The themes and schemes of these festivals were the work and thought of hundreds of clever people marshaled months beforehand to produce one brilliant night.

Florentine preeminence in the production of court shows with dazzling scenic display continued for many years after Buontalenti's career. Giulio Parigi and his son, Alfonso, were Buontalenti's successors. Their work impressed Europe; it was carried and adopted into England by Inigo Jones and into Germany by Joseph Furttenbach. In July of 1637 Alfonso Parigi set up a stage in a courtyard for an opera—*Le nozze degli Dei*. This, our last example of

FIG. 33. *Vulcan's cave,* Le Nozze degli dei, *1637. Alfonso Parigi's setting for Act 2, scene 1, places Vulcan's smithy upstage center with Cyclops about him. Arrows forged by Vulcan are born up to Jupiter by an eagle. Iris appears to tell Vulcan he is to marry Venus. From* The Stage Is Set *by Lee Simonson, published by Theatre Arts Books.*

Medicean magnificence, is worth brief citation. Five composers (for the sake of variety they were five) and 150 singers provided

four hours' pleasure for the ear. Parigi's visual spectacle was varied by no less than fifteen changes of scene as he brought on and off the stage the fantastic geography necessary for the couplings of Jupiter, Juno, Venus, Vulcan, Pluto, Proserpina, Athena, Amphitrite, Diana, and Neptune. The marriage of the gods, indeed.

NOTES

The headnote is from Joseph Furttenbach's *Noble Mirror of Art* of 1663. It is taken from Hewitt's *The Renaissance Stage* (p. 203), where it is translated by George R. Kernodle.

Material in this chapter is chiefly from A. M. Nagler's comprehensive *Theatre Festivals of the Medici*. Other important sources are Bjurström, Campbell, Nicoll, and Strong. Young and Cochrane provided the Florentine background.

The 1586 intermezzi are described in Nicoll's *Development of the Theatre* (p. 93), and the Philander note about *scena ductilis* is given in the same book (p. 91). On p. 73 of Nagler's *Scourcebook* is Vasari's description of San Gallo's perspective scene. That Francesco's embraces were "immoderate" is recorded on p. 129 of Cochrane's study of Florence.

Chapter X

FLORENTINE OPERA AND THE THEATRES AT MANTUA AND PARMA

One cannot grasp the charm and power of his music without having heard him sing it himself. For he . . . is able to convey the total emotional content of the words to the listeners, swaying them at his will to feel joy or lamentation.
— MARCO DA GAGLIANO

The Grand Duke Ferdinando's marriage festival of 1589 marshaled a host of musicians: composers, soloists, choral singers, and instrumentalists. The intermezzi featured five- and six-part madrigals, choruses that have been described as quite imposingly complex, and a finale using seven different vocal ensembles with a total of thirty parts, each part sung by two voices. The musical aspect of the show was as imposing as its scenic spectacle. Yet in Florence at this time, when changeable scenery was introduced, when gorgeous extravaganzas were plied with praise, an aristocratic circle called the *Camerata* was discussing, theorizing, and proposing artistic reforms that contrasted curiously with the superfluities of the court stage and with the florid textured singing then in vogue. In comparison, the aims of the *Camerata* were chaste, their achievements of a quite different kind. Their cynosure was simplicity and it led to the establishment of a new form (some would say bastard form) of theatre—the opera. In the beginning it was not grand opera.

The *Camerata* turnabout from the luxuriance then in the Florentine air came about

because of their interest in the re-creation of the art of Greek tragedy and particularly its musical aspect. The *Camerata* conception that Greek music was simpler than the polyphonic music of their own time was probably correct. However, an exact knowledge of the nature of ancient music must have been as far from their ken as it is from ours, and their notion that Greek tragedy was sustained by continuous music was probably incorrect although closer to the truth than is our notion of Greek tragedy as something much less musical. The *Camerata* concept is yet another example of the pull exerted on the Italian Renaissance artists by their image of the culture of Greece and Rome. They were seeking the resemblance to things past.

A knowledgeable musician and theorist of the group was Vincenzo Galilei, now perhaps better known as the father of the astronomer. Galilei's theoretical discourse on ancient and modern music contained "a declaration of war against counterpoint." Galilei was more apt to praise a piece of music for its effect than for its mathematical correctness. To him the classical ideal required that one voice alone carry the burden of the musical comment on the verse. It was a notion of the *Camerata* that music should adhere to the sentiment of the poet, unelaborated so as not to obstruct the meaning or the enunciation of the words. They were impressed with ancient testimonials to the emotional power of Greek music and hoped to reproduce that effect. One of them, Jacopo Peri, singer, organist, and director of the ducal chapel, expressed their motivating belief that "the Ancient Greeks and Romans . . . used a kind of music more advanced than ordinary speech, but less than the melody of singing, thus taking a middle position between the two."

The *Camerata* musicians advocated, then, a theory that seems strikingly modest in its musicality. In the delightful pastoral play they had a literary type close to a decent libretto, a type that in itself approached music, and their reluctance to pile a musical icing on that cake seems sensible.

It is a bit strange to learn that a sizable number of the prominent members of the *Camerata* labored to wring the musical embellishments of the Florentine intermezzi. Those of 1589, for example, were based on themes supplied by the *Camerata* leader, Count Giovanni de'Bardi, and the overall theme was music. Texts for the intermezzi madrigals were the work of the *Camerata* poet who became what we call a librettist, Ottavio Rinuccini. *Camerata* composers Emilio de'Cavalieri, Giulio Caccini, and Jacopo Peri supplied the music. Peri also appeared and sang as Arion.

In 1597 the first fruits of the *Camerata* discussions and experiments were presented at the house of Jacopo Corsi, who had succeeded Bardi as the group's leader. It was their first presentation and has been regarded as *the* first opera. Called *Daphne,* its text was a pastoral play by Rinuccini, an expansion of an Apollo and Daphne episode in the third intermezzo of the great 1589 festival, and its music was composed

by Peri. This opera was revived at carnival time the next year, 1598, and again in 1599. Its success prepared the way for another work confirming the arrival of the new form, the opera *Euridice,* which had a libretto by Rinuccini and music by Jacopo Peri and Giulio Caccini. Peri sang the role of Orpheus.

Euridice was part of a festival celebrating the marriage of Marie de'Medici (daughter of Joanna of Austria and Francesco de'Medici) to Henry IV of France in October 1600. The theatrical offerings occasioned by this important alliance were dominated by musical works. *Euridice* was staged in the Pitti Palace, and a more spectacular staging of another opera *Il Rapimento di Cefalo* was prepared by Buontalenti in the Uffizi. This was to be Buontalenti's last spectacle.

Opera did not remain Florentine. At Mantua it soon had the enhancing work of musical genius, Claudio Monteverdi. Monteverdi's patron at Mantua was Duke Vincenzo Gonzaga. He was, as his forebears had been, a generous patron of theatrical and musical talent. Like them he had an appetite for magnificence. Vincenzo I was also at times, as princes of this era tended to be, a bit of a brute and more lascivious than most. He liked music, theatre, female performers, and expensive display. In the words of an English "description of the estate of Italie," the duke of Mantua was "given to more delights than all the Dukes of Italye."

The Mantuan court kept up. When Vincenzo married Eleanora de'Medici in 1584, there was an attempt to get the newest thing, a pastoral play. The newest of the moment was Guarini's *Il Pastor fido,* not yet complete but already famous. Guarini sent instead his comedy, *Idropica.* After Vincenzo became duke of Mantua in 1587, he attended the two great Medici marriage festivals in Florence, those of 1589 and

1600. Both times he came home from his sojourn with his in-laws full of ideas. He projected a 1591 production of *Il Pastor fido* to be staged with lavish intermezzi, which may have been canceled because of the death of a Gonzaga cardinal or because, its object being to please Vincenzo's mistress, it displeased his wife. He had his architect build a new theatre. When opera became the latest thing, Vincenzo did not delay long. At carnival in 1607 Vincenzo's *maestro di cappella,* Claudio Monteverdi, presented his first opera. This was *Orfeo,* a work of musical and dramatic unity which the *Camerata* may have wanted but had not as successfully achieved. It brought fame to both court and composer; Mantua surpassed Florence.

The next year Vincenzo's heir, Francesco Gonzaga, married Margherita of Savoy. The predictable fuss included a new opera, a first-class commedia troupe, a *commedia erudita,* intermezzi, and changeable scenery with spectacular machine effects. Duke Vincenzo was patron of the best commedia troupe of the time, Giambattista Andreini's *Fedeli,* and they were called upon to play a revival of Guarini's *Idropica,* which with its intermezzi gave seven hours' wonder to a vast audience. One record would have us believe they numbered 6,000, another says 4,000. A flat wing set presented a prologue, with Mantua, *Idropica's* Padua, and distant realms. There were appropriate settings for the rapes of Proserpina and Europa, for the carryings-on of Jupiter and Alcmena, Hercules and Hebe, and for an assemblage of gods. For variety there were clouds, sea storms, winds, thunders, lightnings, and all that sort of phenomena. Apparently it was not an easy thing for the *Fedeli* to win the attention of the awestruck audience for the prosaic Paduan portion of Guarini's comedy. When an actress searched an actor's pants for a radish, she offended sensibilities happier with amoral myths than with frolick-

ing vulgarity. Whatever reservations the comedians may have been unable to avoid in such surroundings, the theatre, scenes and machines provided for *Idropica* and the intermezzi at least gave the court architect the opportunity to shine. He had to be a born boss as well as an artist as he marshaled his 300 backstage workers to manipulate his machines, cables, and windlasses on cue and without accident.

The leading light of this 1608 festival was Claudio Monteverdi. He composed music for a ballet. He composed the music for the intermezzo-prologue of the comedy which featured a female figure, Manto the founder of Mantua, who "in well-measured movements . . . slowly rose to full height" above the wavy motion of a seascape and then came to stand on the shore of a small island and sang "delicately," enchanting all. Best of all was Monteverdi's new opera, *Arianna.* Its libretto was by the *Camerata* poet Ottavio Rinuccini. Monteverdi provided a lament for Ariadne which was a resoundingly successful aria that brought tears to the eyes of those who heard it. The heroine of this moment was Andreini's wife, Florinda, who appeared in the leading role and "acted with such emotion and in so piteous a way that no one . . . was left unmoved." Of *Arianna,* a Florentine composer who was a contemporary of Monteverdi wrote, "One may truly feel assured that the laudable achievements of ancient music have been renewed."

Monteverdi's contribution to the development of opera now appears to have been crucial. The *Camerata* operas had featured the monodic recitative of Peri and Caccini, had emphasized the text by subordinating the music to it and to its natural rhythm and inflection. Monteverdi enriched the texture, introduced arias, and restored the balance so that the music had a more prominent role. He brought to opera a more flexible musicianship—more variety than the intellectual Florentine composers allowed. He appears to have been less interested in the kind of theory that intrigued them and more attuned to human experience. Was his triumph in part the result of his willingness to ignore the classic past and the top-heavy theories the *Camerata* had built upon it? He focused more surely on human drama. Once he protested the difficulty of composing for a court piece whose *personae* were winds. "Ariadne moved the audience because she was a woman, and equally Orpheus because he was a man and not a wind," he wrote.

The use of flat wing settings for the productions at this Mantuan festival calls for some comment. In the early years of the seventeenth century, the sliding flat wing replaced *periaktoi* as the basic unit or what might be called the building block of the stage setting, just as the *periaktoi* seem to have briefly and in some places replaced the Serlian angle wing. This last (which was first) had two faces, as has been noted: a front face and an angled, perspective face. The stage picture of this Serlian setting admitted some variation, with its cloud machines above and trap work below, and was a pretty vision done up as it was with the so much admired art of perspective painting with decorations, colors, and bright lights. It was even possible, though awkward, to change a setting made up of angle wings. There was a need for quick changes, however, managed in full view of the audience. *A vista* changes, as they were called, were an admired part of the show, one of its most wonderful aspects, and an architect who flunked that part of the job was not contriving as he should. None would have considered hiding scene changes from view with a curtain. Curtains usually hid the stage while the audience assembled; when dropped to reveal the splendor of the scene, that was the end of the use of the curtain. Obviously, *periaktoi* were a means of accomplishing

a vista changes expeditiously. But if they were an ideal means to meet that demand, they made some demands of their own. For one thing, on one flat *periaktoi* surface the painter was required to paint the equivalent of both the front and the perspective face of an angle wing. This flat-faced illusion is a painting problem, and scenery so made is a herald of a long time to come in the European theatre when scene painters rather than architects were the chief backstage artists. The *periaktoi* also made a demand of the stage itself because a setting using the bulky triangular machine needed a deeper, roomier stage space than a setting using angle wings.

The painting skill needed to present architecture, the highly imaginative regions of the interludes on the flat *periaktoi* surface, and the stage depth needed to accommodate *periaktoi* made the sliding flat wing set a logical and an easier next step in scene design. Moreover, the sliding flat wing provided an even tidier, quicker method of making scene changes. Flat wings were arranged in pairs on each side of the stage. As we have seen, it was usual to present an intermezzo followed by an act of the play, another intermezzo, and so on, the play scene returning between times. *A vista* changes conforming to such a scheme could have been managed with the play setting painted on one of the paired flats in place, the intermezzi scenes sliding on to cover the play setting and being pulled off to reveal it and to be changed while in the offstage position. In other words, the intermezzo-prologue represented on one wing of the pair would be pulled offstage and so reveal the comic scene painted on the second wing of the pair. The offstage wing could then be changed while it was out of sight, prepared with a new decoration for the next intermezzo, and then returned to its onstage position at the end of the act. By a constant offstage change of one wing or the other, an

Fig. 34. *Street scene at the eighteenth-century theatre at Drottningholm. This is a photograph of an actual setting of the late eighteenth century preserved at the Swedish court theatre. It shows how painters presented the two visible sides of a building on one flat wing surface. Note how the upper onstage corner of each flat was painted to show a bit of sky, clearly revealed as part of the wing by the harsh lighting used for the photograph. Theatre Arts Prints.*

impressive number of scene changes could be made. There is some evidence, which we may be cordial enough to believe, that Buontalenti's intermezzi scenes of 1589 were mounted on sliding flat wings which were moved onstage to cover the Pisan setting.

The flat wing set has also been credited to the inventiveness of a Ferrarese architect, Giambattista Aleotti. In 1606 Aleotti built the *Teatro degl'Intrepidi* at Ferrara. As far as we know, this was the first theatre designed specifically for wing settings. In this matter there can hardly be a riddle about which came first, the (chicken) wing or the theatre (egg) from which it hatched. Surely the wing set came to light before a theatre was designed specifically for it, whether it was invented by Aleotti or somewhat earlier by Buontalenti or some other un-nominated designer. If this kind of setting was the creation of Aleotti at Ferrara as late as 1606, the employment of flat wings in the settings at Mantua in 1608 is another item that can be added to the list of imitations of the Italian court festivals.

Sliding flat wings came to be manipulated by a chariot and pole. Beneath the stage, in the trap room below on the floor of the hall, a little truck or chariot bore a pole (or a ladder-like rack or frame) which extended up through a slot in the stage floor. The wing was attached to this pole. The slots through which the poles came up from the trap room were, of course, parallel to the curtain line (or on a slight angle to upstage) and were as long as the journey the wings took to get offstage and out of sight. The chariot was pushed or pulled, back or forth, by an attending nudnik in the cellarage who hopefully responded promptly to his cue whenever the wing was to be drawn on or shoved off. His cue was often the musical noise of the intermezzo, and we imagine he had soft soap at hand to lubricate his chariot wheels so that his own noise was not heard.

Another item in the catalogue of imitative court festivals is the building and use of a famous theatre at Parma, an erection of its Farnese prince in 1618. In that year Ranuccio I anticipated a state visit from the Medici Grand Duke Cosimo II. Ranuccio Farnese secured the services of Ferrara's Aleotti to build and equip a large theatre with a capacity of 3,500. Aleotti completed the job and a surviving report made before he left Parma indicates that he had installed and checked out flying machines, wing chariots, a cylindrical screw-shaped machine for sea wave effects, and other devices. The architect also installed a central drum for moving the wings back and forth in unison; that is, a revolving shaft under the stage to which all the wing carriages could be attached by lines of rope so that by turning this central drum all of the paired flat wings would be drawn on and off simultaneously. This device was an improvement over the sometimes uncoordinated response of separate stagehands moving each of the carriages with whimsical individuality. Cosimo II did not visit Ranuccio I in 1618, and for ten years Aleotti's theatre was not used. In the next hundred years it was not used even ten times. Its infrequent use may explain why the *Teatro Farnese* at Parma lasted long enough to be photographed and to be bombed in World War II. Unused theatres are not firetraps. Like Palladio's *Teatro Olimpico,* its very survival made it a snapshot subject and an object of snap interpretations. Theatres also serve that only stand and wait.

What were these snap interpretations? Although this theatre was designed for tournaments and pageantry staged in its large orchestra, although the stage proper was an auxiliary feature, a kind of supplemental addition, the *Teatro Farnese* has been called the first modern theatre. Several things more substantial than an earnest desire to locate that mythical mutant suggest this interpretation. For one, it had a definite proscenium arch in solid architecture. Its elaborate facade, with heavy columns, niches, and statuary, had, like the theatre at Vicenza and unlike the *Olimpico* with its five doors, just one large opening. Also considered modern was the arrangement Aleotti made for flat wing settings, an arrangement that was reflected in theatre architecture for almost three centuries afterwards. Another reason for this interpretation of the *Teatro Farnese* was that its auditorium had a large elongated orchestra surrounded by a steep bank of seats in a horseshoe shape which has been repeated with slight variation in opera houses built until quite recent times. Lately it has seemed as important to train opera glasses on the stage as on the pretty patron opposite, and the sociable, display case horseshoe seems to be vanishing. In

Fig. 35. Teatro Farnese, *Parma. Theatre Arts Prints.*

truth, even though the proscenium, wings, and horseshoe shape may deserve commendation from those who wish to applaud modernity, as part of an exemplary theatre the auditorium was lousy. Only one third of the audience had good sight lines for the stage, and that third was far away from the curtain line. However, Aleotti and his Farnese patron had in mind an exemplary showcase for tournament pageantry, not an exemplary theatre. One final feature of the design reflected in later theatres was the great depth of its stage. It was a far cry, a century away, from the shallow shelf of the perspective stage of Serlian design but an inevitable feature of a stage using flat wings painted to give the illusion of depth. The greater the actual depth, the easier it would be to simulate receding distance, a less forced perspective being more convincing. The inner stage at Parma (the recessed area set at a greater depth) probably not used there for the first time, was another feature copied by many later stages.

Aleotti was past 70 when he built the *Teatro Farnese* at Parma. Though he lived until 1636, another architect was summoned from Ferrara when the theatre finally opened in 1628. This architect was Francesco Giutti. Also brought in from Ferrara to Parma with Giutti was Alfonso Rivarolo, called *Il Chenda,* who later designed settings for opera in Venice. Giutti and *Il Chenda* staged the theatre pieces for a December festival celebrating the marriage of Odoardo Farnese and Margherita de'Medici. A courtyard theatre was the site of a production of Tasso's *Aminta* on December 13. A shivering audience saw it staged with prologue and intermezzi under a cloth rigged to protect its scenic investure from the rain. That the Farnese theatre was not used for this production says something about how useful it was as a theatre. The big theatre had under its roof the gear and rigging for another festival event. One week

later the *Teatro Farnese* was the scene of a tournament spectacular, *Mercurio e Marte.* The stage, with its wing settings and flying machines, made a fine show of contrivance.

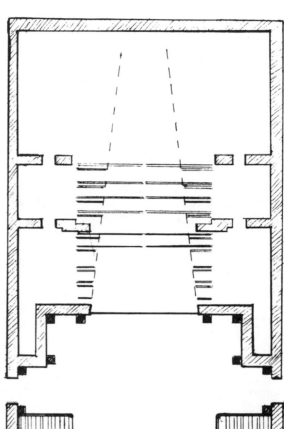

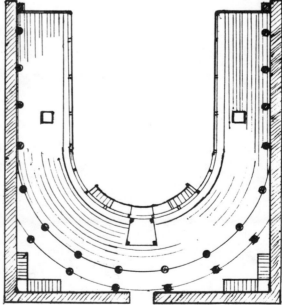

FIG. 36. *Plan of the* Teatro Farnese.

In the large orchestra there was pageantry and a climactic show of monsters, floating islands, ships, and jousting in the arena, which was flooded with water. Claudio Monteverdi, then *maestro di capella* at St. Mark's in Venice and the leading light of the very active musical life of the city, came to Parma with music for *Aminta,* the intermezzi, and the *torneo.*

NOTES

Marco da Gagliano, a Florentine composer, commented on Jacopo Peri's singing in Peri's *Daphne.* The description, used as a headnote for this chapter, is given in Nagler's *Theatre Festivals* (p. 95). It is interesting that Gagliano's own *Daphne,* first produced at Mantua during the carnival of 1608, has been recently revived at the Spoleto and Caramoor festivals of 1973 and at Hunter College in 1974 by the New York Pro Musica Antiqua. Gagliano's further comment that Monteverdi's *Arianna* left him assured that the "achievements of ancient music have been renewed" is given in Nagler (p. 179).

Grout's *Short History* tells of Galilei's "declaration of war against counterpoint" (p. 35) and gives Peri's comment on ancient music (p. 37). The English description of the duke of Mantua is from Lea (p. 343), Schrade's *Monteverdi* gives the detail of the Manto prologue (p. 241), and Arnold's study describes Florinda's singing (p. 21) and gives Monteverdi's objection to composing for winds (p. 116).

Nagler's *Theatre Festivals of the Medici,* the studies of opera by Brockway and Weinstock and by Grout, the studies of Monteverdi by Arnold and Schrade, and Bjurström's book on Torelli were major sources for this chapter.

Chapter XI

SABBATTINI'S STAGECRAFT

I have met with those
That do cry up the machine and the shows;
The majesty of Juno in the clouds,
And peering forth of Iris in the shrouds.
—BEN JONSON

An insight into the methods of Buontalenti, Aleotti, and other architect-stage designers of the time is provided by a book published in 1638, Nicola Sabbattini's *Practica di fabricar scene e machine ne'teatri*, a how-to-do-it guide in two books. Book One dealt with the preparation of a theatre and stage, and the longer Book Two explored the matters of scene changes and the machines used in staging intermezzi. Sabbattini made no claim to inventiveness; he simply recorded what he had seen and done in staging court shows. There is one curious omission. His work, published a good twenty years after the use of sliding wings became frequent, makes no mention of them when changeable scenery is discussed. This has earned him a seat far from the head of the class, where Buontalenti and Aleotti sit— a seat labeled "behind-the-times." He seems to have worked mostly at Pesaro, which was not as solvent as Florence (no city was) nor as given to conspicuous shows. It may be that Sabbattini's practice was more typical than the expensive artifice of Florence, Ferrara, Mantua, or Parma.

An attractive feature of Sabbattini's *Practica* is its illustrations, sketches that have a Rube Goldberg quality with their levers, seesaws, wheels, and other peculiar devices that set things in motion. He wears

out the alphabet using letters to label the parts of his schematic drawings, plopping his ABCs down like a talkative chatterbox who cannot finish a description. Another charm of his book is that as we read we become aware that Sabbattini seems to have been that rarity, a genial technician proud of his work and anxious to share his knowledge. Most of Sabbattini's practice has no immediate application for us—we simply do not do his kind of show—but it's pleasant to dwell in imagination with his problems and see them solved. He appeals to any modern stage designer who has ever had to use his ingenuity. It is as though a companionable spirit has come to his side across three centuries. Sometimes he speaks directly to us, as when he advises the architect to prepare his plan, select good workmen, and then "supervise the work . . . show confidence in all, give good words to all, yet put complete trust in none." If this sounds a bit like a Borgia politician, anyone building a theatre or stage setting today or tomorrow could do no better than to engrave those words on the tablet of his memory. When Sabbattini suggests that scenery might be made of wood rather than of framed cloth, he admits it would "require more time and money" but he speaks the thought of some backstage workers of our time and acquaintance when he adds that scenes so made "are less apt to be damaged by those behind the scenes, especially the thick-headed ones." "Cloth," he adds, "may be easily torn by carelessness." Modern scenic artists live by the same homely wisdom.

Sabbattini's first book, which deals with methods of planning a stage and auditorium set up in a palace hall, is more detailed but not much of a departure from Serlio's treatment. It does not seem that a century of active theatre practice separates these men. Like Serlio, Sabbattini used a raked stage and although his stage had a gentler rake and a greater depth, his scenery is arranged in the manner of Serlian angle wings. He recommends a depth of at least 15 feet and mentions a depth of 20 feet—more than Serlio allowed, but only about half the depth Buontalenti had used at Florence. Sabbattini noted how to lay out architectural features on the perspective face of an angle wing so that it would be painted with correct proportions and diminish in the right way. A generous part of Book One is devoted to chapters whose contents are revealed by their titles, such as, "How to Design the Doors on the Perspective Faces." Similarly, he detailed the intricacies of representing windows, arches, shops, cornices, projections, balconies, and so on.

Sabbattini gave details about the placement of lights onstage. So they would not glare in the eyes of the audience, they were placed behind the houses to light the angle wing house upstage, behind the festoon above in the manner of border lights, and behind a parapet which served as a shield for what we would call footlights. The onstage lamps were mounted on stout beams, which were securely anchored to the floor of the hall and projected upward through holes in the stage floor. So that the movement of scenery or the thumping of dancers would not jar the lights, the holes in the stage floor through which the supporting beams passed were to be cut larger than the thickness of the beams. Moorish dances were popular intermezzo turns and a fire hazard on a lamp-lit scene. For the same reasons, if lights were mounted on the parapet in front of the stage, the parapet was built to stand by itself, independent of the stage. If lights were not mounted on the parapet, it served merely to hide the trap room under the stage and could be fastened to the stage.

Sabbattini began his second book with this sentence: "In the first book we dealt with the method of making scenes and stage devices; now in the second, we shall deal with the *intermezzi,* for today it seems that no good show can be presented without complete or partial change of scenery." This last may have been the understatement of the year 1638. It also suggests that changeable scenery was, in his mind at least, inseparable from intermezzi production. What follows is the best revelation we have of how scene changes were made and how the machinery used in the intermezzi and in opera worked.

Three methods of changing scenes were described, methods which seem a bit awkward in view of the necessity of making changes in full view of the audience. The first seems the most cumbersome method. It involved a change of cloth on the frame of the angle wing; a new cloth painted with the new scene was pulled over the two faces to cover the old scene. The new cloth was gathered at the offstage edge of the front face of the wing. On signal, one or two men ran along a platform placed behind the wing and, with the top corner of the cloth (and the middle of the top edge if two men were used) tacked to a 4-foot stick (or sticks), they drew the new decoration over the old. The best and most dextrous workmen could not have done this very quickly even in the clever way Sabbattini outlined. So we rejoice that his stagecraft included methods by which an audience could be distracted and induced to turn away from the stage. In the moment of distraction, the change was made. A sudden blare of trumpets behind the audience would do the trick, or a mock violent quarrel might be staged in the back of the auditorium to lure attention from the stage. Of course, the more startling and attention-getting, the better. A second method of changing scenes required that a group of angle wings be nested, several close behind the ones in view. There would be as many angle wings in the nest as there were changes to be made. When the show began, the wings used in subsequent scenes were nested and hidden upstage of the visible wing. To make the change, the last (farthest upstage) wing in the nest would be shoved upstage to cover the first angle wing in the nest above. At the conclusion of the show, after all the changes had been gone through, the nest of wings would end up below the wing that had been in view at the start. The first angle wing of the first nest, the one nearest the audience, would not be changed. This unchanging wing could best be used as the vertical member of a proscenium arch bearing no scenic decoration but frankly serving as a frame for the stage picture and incidentally hiding the downstage nest of angle wings. *Periaktoi* were the essential feature of Sabbattini's third method of changing scenes and several notes about their use are given. This he considered the fastest method of scene change. They are fast and they must be rotated quickly, he warned, lest the backstage space be revealed while they are turning. All the *periaktoi* needed to make up the complete scene could be linked to a windlass so that they all revolved together. He notes that if the pivot points of the *periaktoi* were placed off center, a turning of the machines would provide variation in the amount of onstage space—the playing area could be changed with the change to more or less. With

periaktoi it was possible to stage spectacular fires. The painted cloth buildings to be burned were soaked with *aqua vitae* and (there being apparently no seventeenth-century fire marshals or inspectors) a stage-hand stood by this flammable stuff with a candle. At the moment when the building was to burn, the spirits were set aflame and the *periaktoi* revolved and brought on the blaze, an expense of spirits in a waste of flame. When this effect had worked its wonder, the blazing surface was rotated out of sight and its fire doused, we hope.

Sabbattini's stage made use of the *scena ductilis*, or sliding wing upstage of the angle wings, or *periaktoi* composing the scene. The flat backdrop which finished the scene upstage was made in two parts, which could slide off to reveal another scene painted on a flat behind them, or the flat backdrop could be concealed by another set of flat shutters shoved onstage in front of it. If the stage space permitted, these shutters slid off to reveal a recessed, deeper area beyond which was set a scene with a still deeper and therefore more wonderful perspective which seemed to carry the eye far, far away. No doubt this unusual farther distance, appearing after several acts or intermezzi set on a shallower scale, had an enchanting novelty.

The trap work described by Sabbattini was basically simple, although more elaborate arrangements were made as needed. The trap lid cut out of the stage floor was hinged at its upstage edge and fell down when the opposite edge was released by a stagehand below. The ghost, demon, or whatever creature it might have been then came up by means of a ladder, or was lifted up in a handbarrow raised by several stout fellows in the trap room, or a sizable see-saw lever was used to elevate the barrow and do the trick with less sweat. Manto slowly rising from the sea in the Monteverdi intermezzo at Mantua came up by one of these methods. With the trap, it was possible for a character in an intermezzo to appear from nowhere. Dancers grouped in front of the opening trap so that the audience saw neither the trap nor the character come up through it. The trap was then securely closed, the dancers dispersed in a new grouping to reveal the new character, and the audience asked themselves in wonderment where he came from. With slots cut in the floor of the stage, it was possible to effect all sorts of transformations with skillfully painted cutouts being shoved up through the slots to cover the person or thing to be transformed with its new shape. Mythic metamorphoses were so managed. One of Sabbattini's chapters raises expectations of complexity with its title, "How to Make a Ghost or Apparition Appear and Disappear Rapidly In Various Places on Stage." "*Hic et ubique*?" asks the Dane of his father's ghost, "old mole, canst work i' the earth so fast?" What producer would not want to know what Sabbattini promises to tell? The solution is amusingly simple. If there are so many appearances in so many different stage positions, so many slots are cut in the floor and as many painted cutouts of the figure as are needed are made. If the stagehands in the trap room moved and shoved smartly, the trick could be accomplished with just two cutouts. One cutout served if there was enough of an interval between appearances. Several cutouts of varying size were needed if the ghost was to appear at various depths in the perspective setting. Then, the upstage version of the ghost would be made smaller, the downstage cutout "life" size.

Sabbattini's description of the methods of the intermezzi designers in presenting the heavens with their moving clouds and heavenly beings was, again, a description of artful elaborations of simplicity. For this, the heavens were composed of cloth stretched over frames that in cross section were shal-

low arcs suspended above the setting. These arcs were so hung that a gap between them permitted descents and ascents through it and they were positioned and painted so that the gap between them was not apparent to the audience. The painter of the sky sections had to have a delicate mastery of color and tone, for the separate arcs were intended to appear as one expanse of sky. Clouds were painted on similar arcing sections of framed cloth and suspended by poles from a catwalk above the sky pieces. Stagehands aloft in a catwalk maneuvered the clouds by means of the poles that came down through the gap. Sabbattini also described a means of presenting clouds that made use of two large cylinders placed side by side in an opening in the sky. The cylinders were mounted laterally across the stage, were a bit longer than the width of the setting, and were so painted that they matched the nearby sky sections. When they revolved, they brought into view a small painted cloud which grew in size as they continued revolving. A counterrevolution of the cylinders diminished the cloud. Sabbattini seems to have been rather proud of this complicated arrangement. Still another arrangement that provided an expanding or contracting cloud was a variation of the construction of an umbrella.

When it was necessary for gods or heavenly beings to ascend or descend, they were usually mounted on a platform that came up or down through the gap in the sky. A three-dimensional cloud was attached to the platform to conceal it. The cloud moved down or up through the gap, and the sky sections were cut as necessary to permit beams or whatever rigging was needed to pass through. Painted cloth was used to mask the cuts. Winches were used so that great weights could be handled. If a large group, such as the oft-appearing assembly of gods, was to be born aloft, the cloud con-

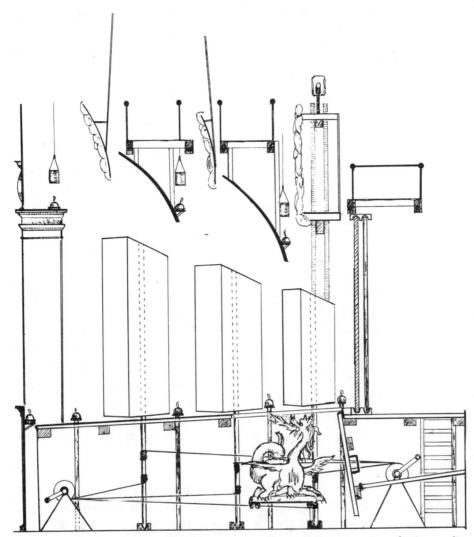

FIG. 37. *Sabbattini's stagecraft. This drawing was made to show intermezzi production as described by Sabbattini. It is hypothetical. Onstage, the* periaktoi *(mounted on pivots and tied to a winch in the trap room) have just begun to revolve to change the scene to a bleak landscape. The trap door has opened, and a fiery monster is about to be lifted up to stage level. The sliding shutters upstage will be pulled apart to reveal a cave painted on the flat above. Clouds will be lowered on poles to cover the arcing sections of the cut heavens, and the lamps up there will be dimmed by metal cylinders lowered to obscure their beams. All will be done in an instant as if by magic. The lamps on the raked stage are mounted on beams projecting through the stage from the floor below. The parapet is free of the stage so that the lamps mounted on it will stand steady. So that the picture will not become too crowded, many supports and beams are not shown. Also not shown are the many men who get in one another's way as they work in the space below, tending lines, turning winches, lifting the monster, propping it in place, and tending the trap and its supporting posts and beams. Inside the monster are two men to animate it and give its firework breath. In the catwalks above, other men maneuver the metal cylinders and the clouds. Others are standing by the rigging of the large elevator upstage. Also undepicted are the chorus waiting in the wings and about to enter to express the woe of a region subject to the monster (a region not ruled by a benevolent duke like the one in the auditorium), the maiden who will enter after the opening chorus to be sacrificed (her lament will make the audience weep), the hero who will slay the monster, the chorus which will descend in the elevator cloud at the end as gods of the finale to celebrate the deed (comparing it to the heroics of the duke in the auditorium), and the instrumentalists who will accompany all of this from galleries erected for them backstage.*

cealing the platform hid what amounted to a large elevator. Yet another method made use of a cosmic see-saw that brought its cloud burden down through the gap and moved it toward the audience. An ascension of this cloud-capped see-saw bore the ascending ones up and away. An iron rod, thin and less conspicuous than a beam needed to bear a comparable weight, was used when it was necessary to lower someone without a masking cloud. Sometimes pasteboard figures in the sky were maneuvered like puppets on thread that was practically invisible. Sabbattini did not detail flying machines, but other architects of this time were using them and could give their flying figures diagonal movement as well as movement up, down, and across. All of Sabbattini's sky motions were straight up and down with the single exception of his see-saw rig. Fully one fourth of Book Two deals with the stagecraft of presenting clouds, the heavens, and the figures therein. This is some measure of what intermezzi producers needed to know. Seascapes with waves and ships and creatures of the deep is another subject of lengthy treatment.

As we read the details of Sabbattini's stagecraft we accumulate a picture of a crowded backstage; we imagine the basement below, the wing space offstage, the loft and catwalks above crawling with an army of stagehands. We are a bit awed with the problems we imagine their proper coordination imposed. We have Sabbattini's word that some could be thick-headed chuffs. Heaven forbid.

The tricks of this stagecraft were often placed upstage, away from the audience, perhaps because their effect depended on the obscuring smoke of the lamps that lit the scene. Engravings of the settings of the time show coherent scenes with gods, clouds, chariots, and whatnots wheeling in the sky without a trace of the rigging, ropes,

harnesses, or platforms we know must have been there. Nor do any visible lines betray the edges of the scenic units that made up the scenes. We cannot see the cuts in the sky. All is whole, all is a unity. Was it so for the audience? Should the effectiveness of the tricks be unquestioned? May we blithely assume the enviable skills that engineers, architects, painters, carpenters, riggers, and devisers brought to the creation of that world of intermezzi magic?

It is hard to imagine that those scenes yielded an illusion comparable to the world outside the theatre, however consistent the elements of that illusion may have been with themselves. For their audience, those scenes must have appeared as a distinct world, a dream world, and tricks were a part of it. The illusion was perhaps conveyed in part by a psychological disposition in its favor and in part by the obscuring haze of candlelight that softened edges and blended the whole. When an actor can be metamorphosed by a pasteboard cutout shoved up a slot in front of him and the slot itself cut in a raked stage, we suspect that more than a painter's skill is involved in the illusion. We suspect that poor visibility is part of it. We have earlier noted Sabbattini's advice about placing "the most beautiful ladies in the middle" of the amphitheatre for the sake of the beneficial effect of their congregated charm on the performers. Apropos of the visual effect of the scenes on the audience, Sabbattini made another note about the seating arrangement. "The persons of culture and taste" were to be seated as close to the distance point, opposite the vanishing point of the perspective, as possible. "They will have the greatest pleasure there, since in such a position all parts of the scenery and the machines are displayed in their perfection, and they will not be able to see the defects which are sometimes discerned by those on the steps or at the sides." In other

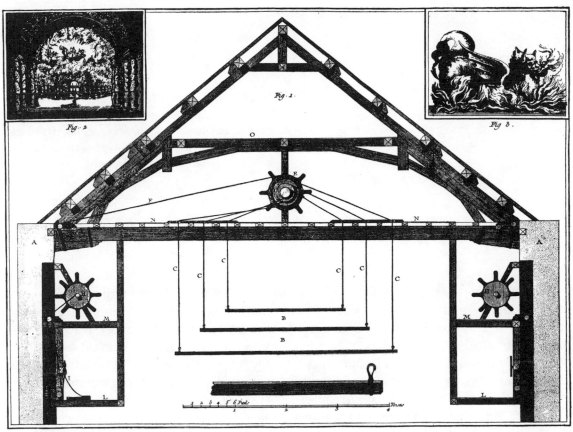

FIG. 38. *Eighteenth-century theatrical machines and the settings they helped to create. (From a French dictionary of the theatre.) Theatre Arts Prints.*

words, the scenes and the sleight of machine did not have to work their magic for all. Those less clearly "of culture and taste" were unlikely to have complained of a less than perfect illusion when the man they courted had paid the bill and had seen something more perfect from the eye point of his own choice seat. One did not rain on the duke's parade. One of the modern stage designer's most vexing problems is to plan the setting so that the poor sight lines from the seats placed at the extremes of the auditorium are taken into account. A modern designer worries about and plans for "those on the steps or at the sides." Sabbattini had

it easier. If the show looked good from the centrally placed throne, he had done well.

NOTES

Ben Jonson's *Expostulation with Inigo Jones* is an eloquent quarrel of a poet with a stage designer and the source of the headnote.

Material in this chapter derives from Sabbattini, translated by John H. McDowell in Barnard Hewitt's *The Renaissance Stage*, published by the University of Miami Press. Direct quotations can be located in this order: pp. 44, 55, 98, 97.

Chapter XII

VENETIAN OPERA

An Opera is a poetical tale . . . represented by vocal and instrumental music, adorned with scenes, machines, and dancing. The supposed persons . . . are generally supernatural, as gods, and goddesses, and heroes . . . .
—JOHN DRYDEN

The story of theatre in Italy has been thus far mostly a story of courtly fun and games indulged in for more than a century. Sabbattini wrote two sentences that cannot be improved upon as a statement of what all this activity was about. "After having made careful selection of the place where the play and the intermezzi are to be presented, the architect must go in person to inspect the site, taking with him good master masons and bricklayers in whom he has confidence, and diligently examine again the capacity of this place. After this the masons will look at the beams, the vaults and the roofs to see if they are sound and able to bear the weight of the stage floor, the machines and the spectators, and especially must this be done when princes are expected in the company." The last phrase implies that one might have cared less about the hazards of production if the prince was not coming to the show, that a prince's presence prevented a collapse of beams, vaults, and roofs, and that without him stage, machines, and spectators could all fall down. To understate the matter, we may say that this was probably not so, and in the same sober style say that to a great extent all depended on the prince. In the auditoriums thrones dominated, and for those dominant thrones the scenes were planned. The intermezzi flatteries were presented to the prince in expensive gift wrappings, in trappings purchased at a rate only he could afford. In stagecraft there was admirable artifice and enviable skill given to a display of magnificent images, conspicuous indications of how much money the prince could spend. By 1600 the Italians had achieved something substantial in some comedies, pastoral plays, and opera. The commedia performers were hustling along their haphazard way. However, a comparison of their lot at the beginning of the seventeenth century with the more firmly established professional players of Spain and England would be odious. The playwrights of those nations were doing more and better than those of Italy. There was princely plenty in this theatre activity, but only the top dogs of a comparatively chaotic Italy had reservations for the show; there were slim pickings for the great unwashed.

If our story is to have a happier ending, it will have to be in an environment where there was some more ease, where there was some treasure to pay the cost, where less exalted, if not common, people could have a regular place, an atmosphere where the whims of princes counted for less. In Italy in the seventeenth century one city had that kind of environment and atmosphere. It was the "Most Serene Republic" of Venice.

Venice was a tourist attraction even in those days. It was renowned for its prostitutes and for its famous carnival. As attractive was the fact that Venice tended to be neutral ground, a sanctuary and refuge, a place to go when fortune waned or welcome wore out at some prince's court. It was a respite from the turmoil of war, a place to flee when it was politic to flee. Venice was a city of about 125,000 people, a commercial city whose ducat was the dollar of the day, and a city ruled by oligarchs who conducted affairs with a minimum of tumult and abrupt shifts in policy. There was a minimum of disruptive struggle. That Venice was declining in power as its trade had declined may cause some historians to shed a tear for vanishing glory. The theatre historian looks at seventeenth-century Venice with a brighter eye, for there the first enduring Italian public theatres were established.

Private theatrical entertainments had been as commonly, if not as expensively, done at Venice as anywhere in Italy. As early as 1565 a theatre, built by Palladio, had been available to the Venetian public. Other theatres were built and several were in use in 1608 when the Englishman Thomas Coryat visited the city. Coryat saw commedia troupes perform, "saw women acte," a thing he had never seen before. He wrote that "noble & famous Cortezans" came to the theatres and that they were accommodated in galleries "on high alone by themselves in the best roome of all the Playhouse," that they were masked and that if a stranger unmasked them "but in merriment only to see their faces" he would be "cut in pieces before he should come forth of the roome." The men in the audience sat in "the yard or court" on stools for which they paid a sum. Aside from the actresses and the hooded harlots, Coryat was not much impressed by his Venetian theatre-going. The theatre seemed to him "very beggarly and base in comparison of our stately Playhouses in England; neyther can their actors compare with us for apparell, shewes and musike." Three decades later a traveler would have found more stately theatrical mansions in Venice.

The significant date in the history of the Venetian stage was 1637, when the *Teatro San Cassiano* opened with the production of *Andromeda,* an opera. This was the year, it will be recalled, of Parigi's lavish Florentine production of *Le nozze degli Dei.* The Venetian opera was not so extravagant a show but rather more important to theatre history because it was the premiere production of the first opera stage open to the general public. It was so successful that two years later two more opera theatres were opened; one of them mounted a long-run revival of Monteverdi's *Arianna.* Still another opera house opened in 1641. In that same year two Monteverdi operas were produced. The next year the supreme music drama of the epoch was presented, Monteverdi's *L'incoronazione di Poppea.* (*Poppea* was in the repertory of the New York City Opera, 1973–74.) After 1650 there were always at least four Venetian opera houses open to the public, and by the end of the century nearly 400 operas had been produced in some seventeen theatres in Venice.

The opera houses and productions were as commercial as the city in which they flourished. Inasmuch as they were business ventures, their success and continuance depended on their appeal to tourists and to common audiences. This had its effect on the operas, their staging, and the architecture of the theatres. The first step in the erection of a public theatre was usually taken by some wealthy family which served as financial backers and sold boxes while the theatre was being built, in that way augmenting the capital invested. A yearly subscription was levied thereafter on the box-holders in order to continue operations. This assured the principal investor a continuing profit each season. A consequence was that every theatre had many balconies and boxes. The *Teatro S. S. Giovanni e Paolo,* built by the Grimani family in 1639, had, for example, five balconies with twenty-nine boxes in each. In addition to the boxes sold on subscription, the theatres had parterre seating that was available to the general public who could buy admission for one performance, the price varying with the demand for seats to a particular production. The performers were Venetian musicians, traveling troupes of singers, and commedia players, and they were paid from the receipts from the parterre seating. There were three seasons when the theatres were open each year. The most important coincided with the Venetian carnival, which ran from immediately after Christmas until Shrove Tuesday. Another began on Ascension Day and continued to the middle of June. An Autumn season ran from September to November.

The operas themselves were fashioned to a paying public's taste. The refined austerities of *Camerata* opera yielded to a more luxuriant indulgence of soloists, whose florid arias became very popular. Before long the operatic chorus virtually disappeared, a development prompted as much by Venetian economics as by Venetian aesthetics. The opera plots blended humor and pathos, became melodramatic, and developed a somewhat incomprehensible complexity. So that the audience could grasp the situation at the start, an *argomento* was provided, a scenario summarized the action scene by scene, and a complete libretto was often published. This public entertainment developed as a rather unrestrained exhibition of an aesthetic that admired complexity above simplicity, that liked the artificial, and that relished actions out of the ordinary.

Venetian opera, as we would expect of a theatre form designed to appeal to a general public, became a thing of spectacle as well as singing. Entertainment was in the spectacle. The stagecraft that had hitherto been the special toy of the court stage became available for the first time to the general public. Opera for the public could not afford as expensive settings as opera for princes, but its investment in scenery was neither slight nor shabby. The tangled melodramas were shaped probably as much by a desire for the wonder-working scenes and machines as they were by an unclassic interest in astonishing stories. One opera librettist frankly said so in a preface declaring that Aristotelian strictures regarding dramatic structure were beside the point; of moment to him were the desires of the inventor of the scenic apparatus and those of the public. This was the declaration of a practical commercial artist, one unhaunted by Roman or Greek ghosts.

The particular inventor of the scenic apparatus referred to was Giacomo Torelli. Torelli was a native of Fano, no great shakes as a theatre town, and it is unknown where he learned his craft. It has been suggested that he worked with Sabbattini at Pesaro or with Giutti at Ferrara, a more likely suggestion. At Venice, Torelli was called *il gran stregone,* the great sorcerer. A story, colorful enough to be told even if untrue, suggests he may have learned the tricks of his trade as the result of an extraordinary compact. According to the story, some Venetian dimwits assaulted Torelli in the street (or did they ram his gondola?) because they were convinced his scenic wizardry was the result of a compact he had made with the devil. His magic was supernatural.

Torelli's first major production on record

was the premiere opera in January 1641 of the fourth Venetian opera house, the *Teatro Novissimo,* which had been planned as "the latest thing," a spectacle showcase. Torelli may have been the architect of this theatre when it was built in 1640. The opera was *La finta pazza*. It concerned Achilles' adventures in Scyrus when he was due to fight at Troy and the feigned madness of Deidamia, which occurred when Achilles turned his thoughts from her. The final solution, not easily arrived at nor without the gods mix-

ing in the mess, was marital for hero and heroine and martial for the hero. *La finta pazza* had a typical Venetian operatic plot, a tangled tale about legendary heroes and gods. As was usually the case in Venetian opera, it had three acts. However scenes and machines were deployed, Torelli was not one to limit *a vista* changes to an act break or even to a scene. *La finta pazza* had harbor, garden, piazza, hell, royal garden scenes, and descents and flights of gods. Within the plot were opportunities for all

FIG. 39. *A setting by Torelli for* La finta pazza. *This* Gran Piazza della città di Sciro *was used for Act 2, scene 8, and for Act 3, scene 4, of the Parisian production of the opera in 1645. Jupiter is surrounded by his court in the heavens above and Deidamia is going mad in the piazza below. From* The Development of the Theatre *by Allardyce Nicoll, published by George G. Harrap & Company, Ltd.*

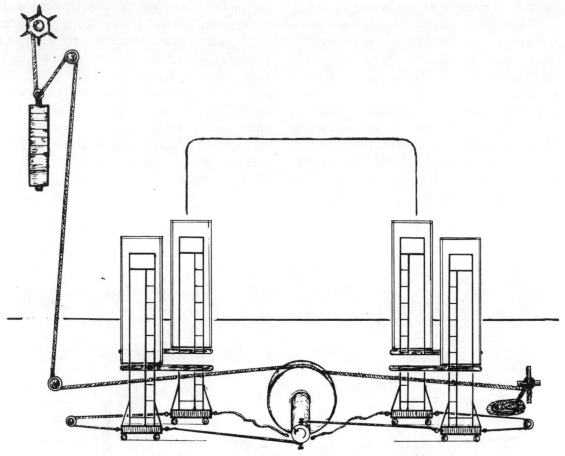

FIG. 40. *This schematic drawing shows how paired wing chariots were moved by a counterweight. The control point is below on the right; the winch is above on the left. The shaft extended the full depth of the stage, so that all the wing chariots could be attached to it, and should be imagined on a lower level—the space immediately below stage was clear for trap work.*

the scenes and machines hitherto marshaled for intermezzi production.

Torelli's machinery moved clouds, gods, and a dragon in diverse directions and sundry ways. But the most impressive features of his staging were the startlingly rapid and complete scene changes he brought off: "*mirabile era l'artificio di questa mutazione.*" It was written that a 15-year-old child could have done the work required for a Torelli scene change. The scenes at the *Teatro Novissimo* were set up on eight pairs of sliding wing chariots deployed on each side of a stage about 32 feet deep. The carriages were linked up by rope to a central

drum, as had been done by Aleotti and other designers, to make sure the sliding wings would all move together when the drum was turned. Torelli's innovation consisted of linking the revolving drum to a counterweight. When this weight was released, it activated the drum and the whole scene moved.

We do not know details of Torelli's scheme, but it probably resembled the counterweight system used to change scenes at the Paris opera in the eighteenth century. There, a winch mounted high on a backstage wall was used to pull up a counterweight that was linked to a control rope.

The control rope passed over a pulley near the winch, ran down to the trap room, passed around the drum in the trap room below the stage, and was attached at a control point. When the change was to be made, the control rope was released at the control point, the weight dropped, the rope pulled, and the drum turned by the rope's passage around it. The wing chariots were arranged in pairs, and the offstage chariot of the pair, linked to the revolving drum by a rope, was pulled on when the drum turned. The paired chariots were linked to each other by another rope, which passed through an offstage pulley in such a way that when the offstage chariot moved on it pulled the onstage chariot off. Preparing this counterweight system for the next change required three operations. The winch pulled the counterweight up. The slack control rope was pulled around the drum and reattached at the control point. The rope of the onstage chariot, which had been linked to the drum for the move onstage, was unlinked and the offstage chariot was hooked up to the drum so that on the next turn of the drum it would be drawn on.

Torelli, stage sorcerer *extraordinaire*, presented eight magnificent scenes and seven sky machine displays in his next carnival season opera, *Bellerofonte*. The next year (1643), for *Venere gelosa*, there were nine distinct settings. In these and other productions Torelli's reputation grew, and in 1645 he was invited to Paris, where he staged *La finta pazza* in December of that year. Although he remained in Paris for sixteen years, Torelli prepared fewer productions there than he had at Venice. The most notable of them was Corneille's *Andromeda* in 1650. French neoclassic ideals acted as a restraint on the proliferation of scenes. Unity of place was prized more than diversity of picture whenever the French wore their theoretical heads. Corneille, for instance, believed that changes should be

limited to the act divisions. Whatever the merits of such thoughts, they were not ideas close to Torelli's heart. In 1661 Torelli returned to his native Fano. There he built the *Teatro della Fortuna* and in 1677 constructed scenery for an opera that was his last work, *Il Trionfo della continenza*. The scenery was an incontinent triumph. Clouds, infernal and celestial regions, a seascape, a square, park, cortile, garden, chamber, gallery, fortress, and royal chamber all came to view.

The stage at Fano had very interesting dimensions. It had thirteen or fifteen paired-wing chariots on each side, disposed along a stage depth of 95 feet. A recessed area behind the shutters at this 95-foot depth

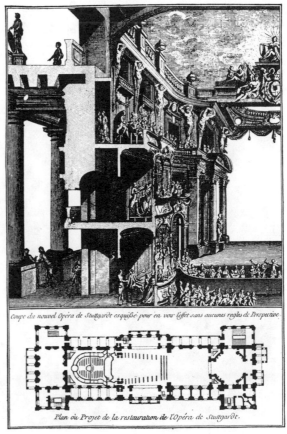

FIG. 41. *Cross section and plan of the Stuttgart opera. (From an eighteenth-century French dictionary of the theatre.) Theatre Arts Prints.*

provided an additional 36 feet with eight more pairs of wings. The full stage depth was a whopping 131 feet. This stage depth is just a bit less than the length of the hall in the Uffizi that contained both stage and auditorium of the *Teatro Medici*. The proscenium width at Fano was 46 feet. Torelli's stage was not unique in its great depth; its dimensions became the ideal for European operatic stages in the late seventeenth century.

Torelli's dimensions illustrate what importance the Italian stage gave to scenic matters. They had little relation to the requirements of opera and less to do with the requirements of drama, but they had everything to do with the enchantment of perspective illusion of distance. On the other hand, libretti were often designed to the requirements of scenic display. Perspective distance exerted a force pulling the very walls of theatres back to a depth where that

illusion of distance could be more easily created. From Serlio's 13-foot depth for a perspective picture, the stage had multiplied its depth ten times. In 1663 the German architect Joseph Furttenbach, in *The Noble Mirror of Art,* wrote an interesting expression of the charm of this kind of illusion. A sympathetic reading disposes us to an imaginative realization of what that delightful thing meant in its day. "What a splendid moving thing is a perspective scene in a theatre. The perspective lines carry the eye so well into the distance that not only the ordinary spectator but the master himself will be carried away against his will and be astonished and entranced." We picture the master sore with the bone-weariness of preparing the show. He has finally gotten his lamps lit and properly placed, and what theatre folk call magic time has come. He "sees it." Furttenbach goes on with these words: "Perspective presents such a lovely

FIG. 42. *A hell scene*, Il pomo d'oro. *The huge monster head framing this scene of inferno recalls the Valenciennes hellmouth of Figure 1. From* The Stage Is Set *by Lee Simonson, published by Theatre Arts Books.*

new world that even a melancholy spirit would be refreshed, strengthened, and persuaded to a longer life."

In Venice the opera sustained by an avid public became an established form of theatre and spread from there to the rest of Europe. As mentioned before, Torelli took his special know-how to Paris. Francesco Cavalli, Monteverdi's pupil who was the leading composer of opera at Venice, was summoned to Paris in 1662 by Cardinal Mazarin to present an opera for the festival marking the marriage of Louis XIV. Pietro Antonio Cesti, another celebrated Venetian composer, went to Vienna to serve the Emperor Leopold. Also to the Austrian court went the stage designer who had been Torelli's chief rival in Venice, Giovanni Burnacini. In Vienna operatic production became the most lavish in Europe. In 1668, when Leopold married the Infanta Margherita of Spain, Cesti composed an opera for the occasion and Giovanni Burnacini's son, Lodovico Ottavio Burnacini, provided the decor. As the Florentine intermezzi of 1589 had been the show of the last century, this Italianate show was the magnificent, expensive display of the seventeenth century. It was *Il Pomo d'oro*. Perhaps its significant action, reflected in its title, was Jupiter's gift of the golden apple to the new empress, an unoriginal conceit with which European royalty had been hit on their crowned heads for as long as there had been entry parades. We are persuaded that from the time of Lucrezia Borgia at Foligno in 1502 to the time of the Infanta Margherita at Vienna in 1668 no princess could bed down with a prince unless, in the humble, frequently voiced, and long-held opinion of her servants in the dramatic arts, she surpassed Aphrodite, Hera, and Pallas Athena. Machinist Lodovico Ottavio Burnacini and musician Pietro Antonio Cesti concocted for this fresh instance an opera of sixty-six scenes, using a total of twenty-four different settings. Further details of this Hapsburg happening may be left to the informed imagination of the reader.

And so, I trust, may a detailed summation of the Italian Renaissance stage. Such a summary would recall the acting of the amateur gentlefolk of the courts, the earliest traveling entertainers, and the professionals who developed the unique commedia dell'arte. It would review the translations and revivals of ancient plays, the writing and performance of Italian plays that hugged the models of Greece and Rome, and the creation of the newer pastoral plays and operas. Some special notice would be given the intermezzi for the scenic and musical developments they promoted by their very being. The perspective stage of Serlio's time and the changeable scenes and machines of Sabbattini's would be remembered, and with them Pellegrino da Udine, Baldassare Peruzzi, Girolamo Genga, and the Florentines who preceded Buontalenti. Palladio's *Olimpico* and the work of Aleotti and Torelli would be reviewed. The *Camerata* would be recalled and Claudio Monteverdi would have special salutation. And dates, pegs on which historians hang their full hats, would come on for a final bow. The year 1486 would be remembered for the sake of the production of *Menaechmi* at Ferrara; 1508, *Cassaria* at Ferrara; 1528, Ariosto's theatre at the Este court; 1573, Tasso's *Aminta;* 1585, *Oedipus* at Vicenza; 1589, the great festival of the Tuscan grand duke; 1604, the death of Isabella and the disbanding of the *Gelosi*; 1606, Aleotti's wing stage at Ferrara; and 1637, public opera at the *Teatro San Cassiano*. In the back of the program there would be a most distinguished patron list: Borgias, Estensi, Medici, and Gonzagas.

As this summary is being made, two unrelated thoughts should dwell in the mind. First, the accomplishments of the Italian stage of this time were exported to the rest of Europe. The commedia, opera, perspective scenes, and changeable scenery came from Italy to the European stage. Second, our history has not been comprehensive. The theatre activity of only some courts and cities and the work of only some theatre artists has been mentioned. A selection has been made to bring the accomplishment of almost two centuries within a brief compass. This could not be done without feeling an unease that is the penalty guilty creatures must suffer in this imperfect world. It is a penalty slightly assuaged by the publication of the bibliography.

FIG. 43. *Design by Lodovico Ottavio Burnacini.* (*From* Monumenta Scenica.) *Theatre Arts Prints.*

NOTES

Dryden's definition of opera is taken from his preface to *Albion and Albanius.*

Sabbattini tells of the need to inspect a theatre site on p. 43 of *The Renaissance Stage,* edited by Barnard Hewitt, University of Miami Press. George R. Kernodle's translation of the Furttenbach appreciation of perspective appears on p. 203 of the same. Coryat is quoted from Nagler's *Sourcebook* (p. 259). Bjurström records on p. 109 that *"mirable era l'artificio"* of Torelli's scene changes.

Bjurström's study of Torelli includes material on Venice and Venetian opera, of which I have made heavy use. Other sources are the books on Monteverdi and on opera cited in the notes to Chapter X. The Hawley and Jackson article listed in the bibliography provided the technical information on the counterweight system.

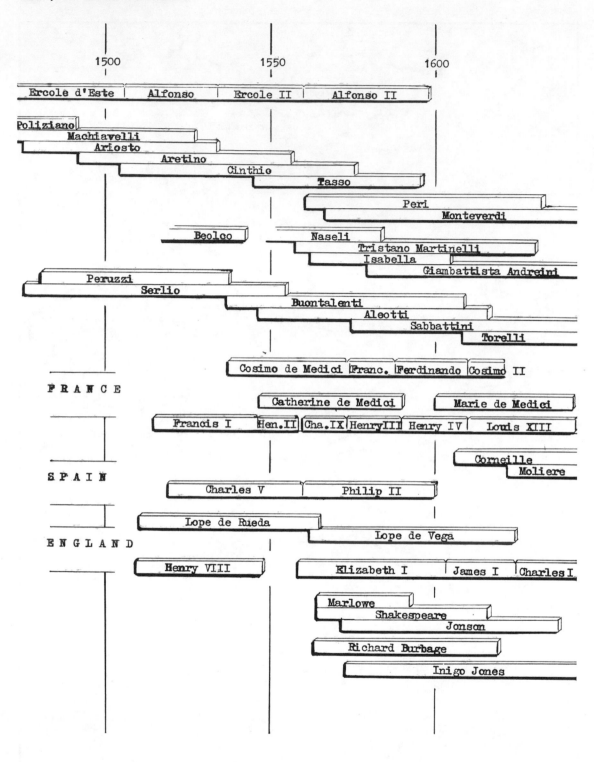

Arnold, Denis. *Monteverdi.* London, J. M. Dent and Sons, Ltd., 1963.

Beare, W. *The Roman Stage, a Short History of Latin Drama in the Time of the Republic.* Cambridge, Mass., Harvard University Press, 1951.

Beijer, Agne. "An Early 16th-Century Scenic Design in the National Museum, Stockholm, and Its Historical Background," *Theatre Research,* Vol. IV, No. 2, 1962.

Bellonci, Maria. *The Life and Times of Lucrezia Borgia.* Trans. by Bernard and Barbara Wall. New York, Pyramid Books, 1973.

Bjurström, Per. *Giacomo Torelli and Baroque Stage Design.* Stockholm, Almqvist & Wiksell, 1962.

Brockway, Wallace and Herbert Weinstock. *The Opera, A History of Its Creation and Performance.* New York, Simon and Schuster, 1941.

Campbell, Lily B. *Scenes and Machines on the English Stage During the Renaissance.* New York, Barnes and Noble, Inc., 1960.

Cartwright, Julia. *Isabella D'Este.* New York, E. P. Dutton & Co., Inc., 1903.

Cheney, Sheldon. *The Theatre.* New York, David McKay Company, Inc., 1952.

Clark, Barrett H., ed. *European Theories of The Drama.* Rev. ed. New York, Crown Publishers, 1947.

Cochrane, Eric. *Florence in the Forgotten Centuries, 1527–1800.* Chicago and London, The University of Chicago Press, 1973.

Ducharte, Pierre Louis. *The Italian Comedy.* Trans. by Randolph T. Weaver. New York, The John Day Company, 1929.

Duckworth, George E. *The Nature of Roman Comedy, A Study in Popular Entertainment.* Princeton, New Jersey, Princeton University Press, 1952.

Freedley, George and John A. Reeves. *A History of the Theatre.* New York, Crown Publishers, Inc., 1955.

Gardner, Edmund G. *Dukes and Poets in Ferrara.* London, Archibald Constable & Co., Ltd., 1904.

————. *The King of Court Poets.* London, Archibald Constable & Co., Ltd., 1906.

Gassner, John. *Masters of the Drama.* New York, Dover Publications, 1945.

Gassner, John and Ralph G. Allen. *Theatre and Drama in the Making.* Boston, Houghton Mifflin Company, 1964.

Gilbert, Allan H., trans. & ed. *Machiavelli; The Prince and Other Works.* Chicago, Packard and Company, 1941.

Gilder, Rosamond. *Enter the Actress.* New York, Theatre Arts Books, 1960.

Gorelik, Mordecai. *New Theatres for Old.* New York, E. P. Dutton & Co., Inc., 1962.

Greg, Walter W. *Pastoral Poetry & Pastoral Drama.* London, A. H. Bullen, 1906.

Grout, Donald Jay. *A Short History of Opera.* 2nd ed. New York and London, Columbia University Press, 1965.

Hartnoll, Phyllis, ed. *The Oxford Companion to the Theatre.* 2nd ed. London, Oxford University Press, 1957.

Hawley, James and Allen S. Jackson. "Scene-Changing at the Palais Royal (1770–1781)," *Bulletin, Ohio State University Theatre Collection,* No. 8, 1961.

Herrick, Marvin T. *Italian Comedy in the Renaissance.* Urbana, The University of Illinois Press, 1960.

————. *Italian Tragedy in the Renaissance.* Urbana, The University of Illinois Press, 1965.

Hewitt, Barnard, ed. *The Renaissance Stage, Documents of Serlio, Sabbattini, and Furttenbach.* Coral Gables, Florida, University of Miami Press, 1958.

Kennard, Joseph Spencer. *The Italian Theatre.* New York, William Edwin Rudge, 1932.

————. *A Literary History of the Italian People.* New York, The Macmillan Company, 1941.

Kernodle, George R. *From Art to Theatre, Form and Convention in the Renaissance.*

Chicago, University of Chicago Press, 1944.

Laver, James. *Drama: its Costume and Décor.* London, The Studio Publications, 1951.

Lea, K. M. *Italian Popular Comedy.* Oxford, Oxford University Press, 1934.

Mazzone-Clementi, Carlo. "Commedia and the Actor," *The Drama Review,* Vol. 18, No. 1 (T-61), March, 1974.

Mumford, Lewis. *The City in History.* Hamonds Worth, Middlesex, England, Penguin Books, 1961.

Nagler, A. M. *A Source Book in Theatrical History.* New York, Dover Publications, Inc., 1959.

——. *Theatre Festivals of the Medici.* New Haven and London, Yale University Press, 1964.

Nicoll, Allardyce. *The Development of the Theatre.* 4th ed., rev. New York, Harcourt, Brace & World, Inc., 1957.

——. *Masks, Mimes and Miracles.* London, George G. Harrap & Co. Ltd., 1931.

——. *Stuart Masques and the Renaissance Stage.* London, George G. Harrap & Company, Ltd., 1937.

——. *The World of Harlequin.* Cambridge, Cambridge University Press, 1963.

Niklaus, Thelma. *Harlequin, or The Rise and Fall of a Bergamask Rogue.* New York, George Braziller, Inc., 1956.

Noyes, Ella. *The Story of Ferrara.* London, J. M. Dent & Co., 1904.

Oreglia, Giacomo. *The Commedia dell'Arte.* Trans. by Lovett F. Edwards. New York, Hill and Wang, 1968.

Orgel, Stephen and Roy Strong. *Inigo Jones: the Theatre of The Stuart Court.* Los Angeles, University of California Press, 1973.

Power, Eileen. *Medieval People.* Boston and New York, Houghton Mifflin Company, 1935.

Prezzolini, Giuseppe. *The Legacy of Italy.* New York, S. F. Vanni, 1948.

Schrade, Leo. *Monteverdi, Creator of Modern Music.* London, Victor Gollancz, Ltd., 1964.

Simonson, Lee. *The Art of Scenic Design.* New York, Harper & Brothers Publishers, 1950.

——.*The Stage Is Set.* New York, Theatre Arts Books, 1963.

Smith, Winifred. *The Commedia dell-Arte.* New York, Benjamin Bloom, Inc., 1964.

——. *Italian Actors of the Renaissance.* New York, Coward-McCann, Inc., 1930.

Southern, Richard. *The Seven Ages of the Theatre.* New York, Hill and Wang, 1961.

Strong, Roy. *Splendor at Court.* Boston, Houghton Mifflin Company, 1973.

Symonds, John Addington. *The Renaissance in Italy.* New York, Henry Holt and Company, 1888.

Wiley, W. L. *The Early Public Theatre in France.* Cambridge, Mass., Harvard University Press, 1960.

Young, Col. G. F. *The Medici.* London, John Murray, 1920.

Margherita, Infanta of Spain 117
Margherita of Savoy 97
Maria of Austria, Empress 76
Marivaux, Pierre 69
Marlowe, Christopher 74
Martelli, Camilla 81
Martinelli, Drusiano 67
Martinelli, Tristano 55, 67
Masks 57, 58, 59, 60, 61, Figs. 4, 15, 17, 20, 21, 22, 24
Mazarin, Cardinal 117
Medici, Alessandro de 86
Medici, Catherine de, Queen of France 64, Figs. 3, 15
Medici, Cosimo de 81, 86, 87, 90
Medici, Cosimo II 99, Fig. 29
Medici, Eleanora de 96
Medici, Ferdinando de 66, 91
Medici, Francesco de 81, 90, 91, 95, 96, Fig. 32
Medici, Margherita de 101
Medici, Marie de, Queen of France 55, 66, 67, 96, Fig. 25
Medici, Virginia de 81
Medicine show 53
Menaechmi 21, 25, 26, 27, 28, 29, 30, 32, 33, 38, 81, 117
Mercurio e Marte 101
Mercutio 60
Milan 70
Milan, Lodovico il Moro, Duke of 28
Miles Gloriosus 22, 60
Mimes 17, 50, 51
Minturno, Antonio Sebastiano 35
Mirtilla 67
Molière 37, 56, 60, 69, Fig. 14
Monteverdi, Claudio 97–98, 102, 105, 111, 117
Moretti, Marcello 70
Morse, Robert 70
Moryson, Fynes 49
Mountebanks 49, 50, 53, Fig. 16
Multiple staging 15–16, 31, 87, Fig. 1
Munich 51, 52
Mussato, Albertino 31
"My Last Duchess" 24

Naples 61
Naseli, Alberto 51, Fig. 15
Nashe, Thomas 68
Negromante 29
Neroni, Bartolomeo 43
Nicholas V, Pope 38
Noble Mirror of Art, The 116
Nozze degli Dei, Le 94, 111, Fig. 33

Oedipus 76, 82, 117
Olivier, Sir Laurence 58
Olympic Academy 76, 79
Opera 31, 72, 81, 94, 95–98, 104, 110, 111–115, 117
Orange Bowl, The 87
Orbecche 34, 62

Orchestra 39, 44, 76, 100, 102
Orfeo 97
Orlando Furioso 28
Ortensio, L' 43
Over Here! 14

Padua 29, 31, 34, 51, 67
Pageantry 21, 25, 36, 90, 100, 102
Painting 27, 29, 40, 44, 88, 98, 106, 108
Palazzo Vecchio 90
Palladio, Andrea 76–79, 82, 100, 111, 117
Pantalone 53, 57, 59, 60, 65, 67, 69, Figs. 15, 18, 20, 21
Panzanini, Gabrielle Figs. 17, 20
Pappus 50
Parapet 104, Figs. 29, 37
Parigi, Alfonso 94, Fig. 33
Parigi, Giulio 94
Paris 41, 51, 64, 65, 66, 69, 115, 117
Parma 99–101, 103
Parolles 59
Pasquati, Giulio 65, Fig. 20
Pastor fido, Il 74, 96, 97
Pastoral Play 31, 46, 62, 65, 67, 72–75, 96, 97, 101, 110, 117, Fig. 25
Pavia 28
Pazzia, La 66, 92
Pedrolino 54, 61, 68
Pellegrina, La 92–93
Pellegrino—see Udine, Pellegrino da
Pellesini, Giovanni 68
Peri, Jacopo 96, 97
Periaktoi 78, 85, 88, 90, 92, 98, 105
Perspective 27, 40
Perspective face—see Angle wings
Peruzzi, Baldassare 41, 43, 117, Fig. 8
Pesaro 103, 112
Petrarch 31, 51, 67
Philander (Guillaume Philandrier) 85
Piazza della scena, La 44, 86
Piccolo Teatro (Milan) 70
Pierce Pennilesse 68
Pierrette 15
Pierrot 15, 61, Fig. 21
Piissimi, Vittoria 68, 91, 92
Pippin 14
Pistol 59
Pitti Palace 96
Plautus 21, 22, 24, 25, 26, 27, 28, 29, 30, 32, 33, 36, 40, 45, 59, 81, 117
Politics 20, 23, 28, 36, 38
Poliziano, Angelo 31, 36
Polo, Zan 51
Pomo d'oro, Il 117, Fig. 42
Ponti, Diana 67
Popes 20, 21, 28, 38, 41, 44
Population figures 24, 81, 111

Porbus, Paul Fig. 15
Practica di fabricar scene e machine ne' teatri 103
Prince, Hal 16
Prisciani, Pellegrino 26, 38
Professionalism 23, 29, 54–55, 64
Progne 32, 62
Proscenium 14, 43, 72, 78, 100, 105
Pulchinella 61
Punch 15, 61

Raked stage 42, 77, 104, Fig. 37
Raleigh, Sir Walter 74
Ramponi, Virginia 68
Raphael 44
Rapimento di Cefalo, Il 96
Rasser, Johann Fig. 2
Ravenna, battle of 28
Razullo Fig. 22
Re, Maphio dei 51
Regole generali di architettura 41
Religious theatre 15–17, 26, 64, 90
Renee of France 28
Rinuccini, Ottavio 96, 97
Rivarolo, Alfonso 101
Rochester (Eddie Anderson) 54
Roman academy 32
Roman drama—see Plautus, Seneca, Terence
Roman theatre 38–39, 78
Rome 20–21, 24, 28, 32, 41, 50, 51, 87
Roncagli, Silvia Fig. 20
Roscius (Quintus Roscius Gallus) 51
Rosse, Herman Fig. 9
Rotari, Virginia 68
Ruzzante—see Beolco, Angelo

Sabbattini, Niccolo 45, 103–109, 110, 112, 117, Fig. 37
Sacrifizio 73
Salviati, Francesco 88
San Gallo, Bastiano da 86–88, 91
Sancho Panza 60
Savonarola 39
Scaena—see Scenic façade
Scaena ductilis—see Shutters
Scaena versatilis—see *Periaktoi*
Scala, Flaminio 68
Scaliger, Julius Caesar 34, 35
Scamozzi, Vincenzo 77–78, 79
Scapin 60
Scapino 61
Scaramuccia 64
Scenarios 55–57, 68, 70
Scene changes—see Changeable scenery
Scenery 20, 26–27, 38, 40–41, 42–43, 45–47, 69, 77, 82–83, 85–95, 97, 98–100, 103–109, 112–116
Scenic façade 39, 78
School for Husbands, The Fig. 14
Scolari, Baptista 53

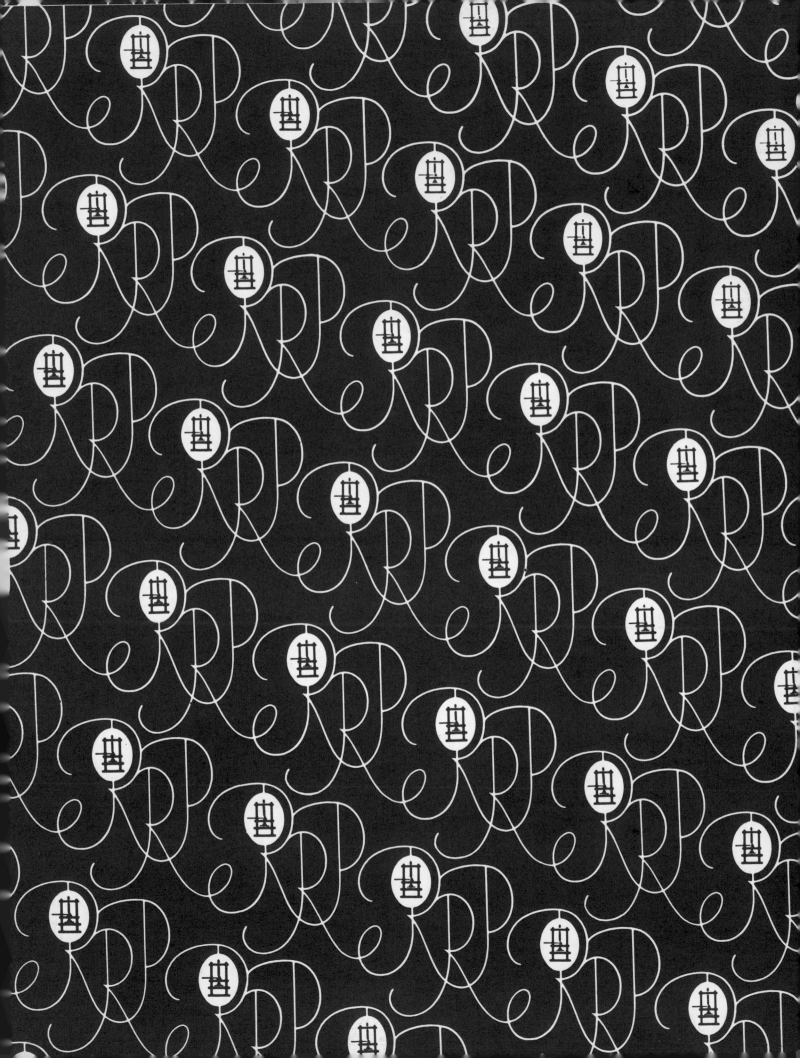